An Annotated Bibliography
of Greek and Roman Art,
Architecture, and Archaeology

Garland Reference Library of the Humanities (Vol. 28)

An Annotated Bibliography
of Greek and Roman Art,
Architecture, and Archaeology

William D.E. Coulson

Garland Publishing, Inc., New York & London

1975

Copyright © 1975

by William D. E. Coulson

All Rights Reserved

Library of Congress Cataloging in Publication Data

Coulson, William D   E   1942-
   An annotated bibliography of Greek and Roman art,
architecture, and archaeology.

   (Garland reference library of the humanities ;
v. 28)
   1. Art, Classical--Bibliography. 2. Classical
antiquities--Bibliography. I. Title.
Z5932.3.C68 [N5610] 016.709'38   75-24081
ISBN 0-8240-9984-2

Printed in the United States of America

Contents

Introduction

This bibliography has been written with four types of readers in mind: the general reader, who may find here books of a non-technical nature for his own enjoyment; the teacher, who will find here not only books recommended as texts for class use but also those suitable for supplementary reading; the undergraduate, who may find here books that will aid him in writing papers or in studying for examinations; and, the graduate student who will find in the appendices books of a specific nature on individual topics. An attempt has been made to include in this bibliography all the paperbacks still in print that have been published by American publishers. Some hardbacks have been included. The criteria for including these books are twofold: (1) those books which are of a sufficiently general nature so as to be recommended either for use as a text for undergraduate classes or for supplementary reading, and (2) those books which are $10.00 or under (with a few exceptions), as being within the price range for students. Hardbacks above $10.00 of a more specific nature, useful to both the student and the specialist, have been included in an appendix. A discussion of important German and French books and periodicals still in print (useful to the graduate student) is included in another appendix. And, due to current interest in urbanism and urban planning, an appendix on this subject in the Greco-Roman world has also been added at the back.

At the end of the comments for each entry, a letter symbol has been placed, designating the suitability of the book. The explanation of these letters is as follows:

A. Recommended for use as a text for undergraduate classes.
B. Recommended as supplementary reading for undergraduates.
C. Useful as a teacher reference, but not recommended for student reading.

INTRODUCTION

For the sake of clarity, this bibliography has been divided into seven sections, each comprising one important area, and three appendices:

I.   Works of a general nature covering both Greek and Roman art, architecture, and archaeology.
II. The aims, methods, and history of archaeology.
III. Prehistoric Greek archaeology.
IV. Archaic, Classical, and Hellenistic Greek art, architecture, and archaeology.
V.   The Etruscans.
VI. Roman art, architecture, and archaeology.
VII. Miscellaneous.

Appendix 1. Ancient Urbanism and Urban Planning.
Appendix 2. Useful hardcover editions above $10.00.
Appendix 3. Important German and French books.

A word should be mentioned about the publication data given in this bibliography. Books today, especially paperbacks, drift in and out of print and regularly shift from one publisher to another. The past few years have also seen marked increases in the prices of books, and the prices quoted in the bibliography might well have changed in the time that has elapsed between writing and printing. For the very latest details, the reader is urged to consult the most recent issue of *Books in Print,* which can be found in most major bookstores and libraries.

I. GENERAL

There are relatively few books in this area. What is needed is a
good treatment of Greek and Roman art and archaeology in one
paperback volume where the Roman part is treated with the same
care and depth as the Greek half.

BOHR, R.L. Classical art. (Art Horizons.) Dubuque, Iowa: Wm. C. Brown
Co. 1968. Pp.158; 89 ill. $2.25 paper.

A handbook of Greek and Roman aer and architecture, written in
outline form. Students in an introductory undergraduate course may
find this book useful, since it presents a valuable synopsis of
the main trends and styles of Greek and Roman art. Copious plans
and charts attempt to bring order to the various periods, and
the author limits himself to a discussion of only the most famous
works from each period. Two major criticisms, however, must be
considered. First of all, the focus of the book seems to be on
Archaic and Classical Greek art and architecture, thus giving a rather
unbalanced view of the history of Greek art. Minoan and Mycenaean
archæology is dismissed in eight pages, and there has been no
attempt to discuss the importance of either the Minoans or the
the Mycenaeans. On the other side, the Hellenistic period receives
only seven pages. The developments of secular architecture,
city-planning, and the private house are barely mentioned. The
author simply calls attention to the Bouleuterion at Miletus and
House XXXIII at Priene, but nowhere provides plans of these
buildings or discusses their significance. Again, perhaps one of
the greatest sculptural monuments of the Hellenistic period, the
Pergamene altar frieze, is dismissed in two sentences with no
accompanying illustrations. Lastly, mosaics and their development

are completely neglected. Second of all, in the Roman part of
the book, the concentration seems to be largely on architecture.
Roman painting and its importance is glossed over, and the field
of mosaics is not even mentioned. If these caveats are kept in
mind, this book can serve as a good outline introduction to Greek
and Roman art and architecture. B.

BROOKS, A.M. Architecture. (Our Debt to Greece and Rome Series.)
New York: Cooper Square 1963. Pp.189. $3.50 cloth.

   First published in 1924.

A very sketchy and inconclusive treatment of Greek and Roman
architecture. The author discusses in very general terms many
of the major religious monuments, but fails to treat domestic
architecture, public buildings, and city planning. The book is
also confusing in that it does not include a single plan,
photograph, or drawing. C.

COARELLI, F. Greek and Roman jewellery. (Cameo Series.) New York:
Tudor Publishing Co. 1970. Pp.157; 68 pls. $2.95 cloth.
Primarily a pictorial survey of Greek and Roman jewellery. Each
of the sixty-eight color plates contains a short paragraph of
description. A rather short and sketchy introductory text runs
throughout the book. There is no correlation between text and
plates. B.

COTTRELL, L. The anvil of civilization. New York: The New American
Library 1957. Pp.256; 22 pls.; 13 ill. $1.25 paper.
A popular archaeological history of the early civilizations in the
Mediterranean, including the Egyptians, Hittites, Sumerians,
Assyrians, and Babylonians. In addition, the author devotes one
chapter to Minoan Crete, one to Mycenaean Greece, and another to

Classical Greece. It should be emphasized that these chapters
are not scholarly in nature and only give the barest of historical
facts. There is, however, plenty of amusing anecdote which makes
for pleasant reading. Because of its popular nature, this book is
not recommended for class use, other than for the briefest of
supplementary readings. B.

COTTRELL, L. The Horizon book of lost worlds. New York: Dell Publishing
Co. 1964. Pp.383. $.75 paper.

First published in 1962.

A popular account, intended for the general reader, of the discovery
of nine civilizations of antiquity, including, amongst others, the
Minoan, the Mycenaean, and the Etruscan. B.

FINLEY, M.I. Ancient Sicily to the Arab conquest. New York: Viking
Press 1968. Pp.226; 12 pls.; 8 ill. $7.50 cloth.

A much needed general account of the history of ancient Sicily.
This is the first book in English to incorporate the new archaeological
discoveries of the past two decades. The author is at his best when
he is talking about Sicily in the Fifth and Fourth Centuries B.C.
and again under Roman rule. Prehistoric and archaic Sicily, on
the other hand, receive sketchy treatment. For instance, he does
not discuss the ancient sources on the proto-history of the
island, nor the connections between Sicily and the Aegean in the
Bronze Age. Perhaps the greatest gaps occur in the treatment of
the Greek colonization of the island. Nowhere does the author discuss
the theories for the cause of this colonization, nor the problems
concerning the foundation dates for the colonies themselves and the
discrepancies between the Thucydidean and Timaean chronologies.

He also neglects to discuss the extent of the Greek penetration
inland and of how the recent archaeological discoveries,
especially those at Morgantina and adjacent sites, have shown
the extent of Greek expansion towards the center of the island.
At the other end of the pole, the author dismisses Byzantine
Sicily in eleven pages. There is no good modern account of
Byzantine Sicily, and the author has missed his chance to
provide one. This is primarily a history book, and the reader
will not find in it many plans and photographs. B.

FLEMING, J., HONOUR, H. and PEVSNER, N. The Penguin dictionary of
architecture. Baltimore: Penguin 1966. Pp.248; 86 ill.
$1.95 paper.

An excellent general reference work on architecture. Greek and
Roman terms and buildings are included in their appropriate
places in the alphabetical listing. Useful to the general reader,
student, and specialist. B.

GROENEWEGEN-FRANKFORT, H.A. and ASHMOLE, B. The ancient world.
(The Library of Art History, vol.1.) New York: The New American
Library 1967. Pp.304; 104 pls.; 38 ill. $1.25 paper.

A well-written general survey of art and architecture in the
ancient world from the beginnings in Egypt and Mesopotamia to the
end of the Roman empire. This book concentrates upon Greek art
and architecture. Especially weak is the chapter on Mesopotamia,
in which the art and architecture of the various civilizations of
the Euphrates are discussed only in the most general terms without
many illustrations and plans. Assyrian architecture is especially
neglected. The chapters on Greek art are generally excellent, but
the chapter on the Hellenistic period could be expanded to include

a fuller discussion of painting and mosaics. The section
on Cyprus consists of only three pages; this important island
needs a far more comprehensive treatment. The major caveat,
however, occurs with the chapter on Roman art and architecture.
The concentration here seems to be on the architecture at the
expense of painting, mosaics, and to some extent sculpture.
For instance, the authors dismiss the whole history of Roman
mosaics in one short paragraph and nowhere do they include
illustrations of mosaics. Likewise, in the field of sculpture,
the great classicistic revival under Hadrian is largely neglected,
as is the art and architecture of the late Roman empire.
Students may find this book useful, but should realize that this
is neither a comprehensive nor a balanced treatment of the art
and architecture of the ancient world. B.

HILL, G.F. Ancient Greek and Roman coins: a handbook. Chicago:
Argonaut 1964. Pp.302; 16 pls.; 31 ill. $10.00 cloth.

First published in 1899.

An old but still useful handbook of Greek and Roman coins. The
author begins with a general sketch of the history of coinage in
Greece and Rome and then proceeds to discuss the metals used,
monetary theory and practice, the classification of coin types,
the explanation of inscriptions and mint marks, and the dating
of coins. B.

-8-

HOPE, T. <u>Costumes of the Greeks and Romans</u>. New York: Dover Publications 1962. Pp.348; 300 ill. $2.50 paper.

First published in 1812.

A comprehensive collection of 300 engravings originally copied from ancient vases and statuary by Thomas Hope (1770-1831), a British designer. In addition to the costumes, there are interesting engravings of musical instruments, articles of furniture, and women's jewellery. B.

JEX-BLAKE, K. and SELLERS, E. <u>The elder Pliny's chapters on the history of art</u>. Chicago: Argonaut 1968. Pp.252. $10.00 cloth.

First published in 1896.

This is still the best treatment of Pliny the elder's chapters from the <u>Natural History</u> (34-36) on sculpture and painting. An English translation faces the Latin text. This is far better than the Loeb edition because it contains not only notes in the margin beside the text but also an archaeological and artistic commentary at the bottom of every page. The introduction contains a long discussion of Pliny's sources. A supplementary bibliography (1897-1966) has been added at the beginning by the Rev. R.V. Schoder to bring the reader up to date. C.

KAHANE, P.P. <u>Ancient and classical art</u>. (20,000 Years of World Painting, vol. 1.) New York: Dell Publishing Co. 1967. Pp.203; 172 ill. $1.45 paper.

An illustrated history of painting from Prehistoric cave

painting to late Roman mosaics. After a brief introduction,

the book consists of color plates, chronologically arranged,

and under each of these there is a commentary. Greek painting

is covered thoroughly, but late Roman painting and mosaics

are completely neglected. B.

KARAGEORGHIS, V. The ancient civilization of Cyprus. New York:

Cowles Book Co. 1969. Pp.259; 181 pls. $10.00 cloth.

A reissue of the Cyrpus volume in the Archaeologia Mundi

series, which has been out of print. This is an important

and welcome volume on the archaeology of Cyrpus, an area

which has been sadly neglected. Two caveats must be kept in

mind. The author devotes the majority of his text to Neolithic

and Bronze Age Cyprus and dismisses the Classical,Hellenistic,

and Roman periods in thirty pages. Secondly, there is not a

single plan in the entire text, often causing the reader con-

fusion. The book, however, is valuable for its chapters on

the Bronze Age and for its excellent photographs. B.

KJELLBERG, E. and SÄFLUND, G. Greek and Roman art. New York:

Thomas Y. Crowell Co. 1970. Pp.250; 192 pls.; 58 ill. $4.95

paper.

　　First published in 1968.

A well-written survey of Greek and Roman art and architecture.
The authors discuss separately the architecture, painting, and
sculpture of each individual artistic period. The Greek part
of the book is weighted to the side of sculpture at the expense
of architecture. For instance, the few pages devoted to the
Geometric period are inadequate. These could stand revision
in regard to Geometric architecture and expansion to include
figurines and jewellery. The architecture of the Athenian
Acropolis is, of course, discussed, but the equally important
Agora in Athens is completely neglected (the authors do not
even include the Hephaesteum and its sculptures). In the
Roman part of the book, the emphasis is placed on the period
from Augustus to Septimius Severus. Indeed, after a far too
brief (ten pages in length) chapter on the Etruscans, the
authors begin talking about the age of Augustus, completely
passing over the early occupations on the Palatine and the major
examples of Republican architecture and sculpture. Similarly,
the section on late antiquity needs considerable expansion to
give balance to the rest of the book. The work is clearly
written, and with the above reservations it can be used as a
class text. A.

KURZ, O. Fakes, 2nd ed. rev. New York: Dover Publications
1967. Pp.348; 142 ill. $2.75 paper.

First published in 1948.

Perhaps the most comprehensive work on art fakes in English.
The author encompasses the entire field of art forgeries;
various forgeries of Greek and Roman works are discussed
throughout the book. The author has added a new appendix of
fakes which have become known since 1948. B.

MAIER, F.G. Cyprus. New York: Fernhill House 1968. Pp.176;
    8 ill.; 6 maps. $4.50 cloth.

A very readable history of Cyprus from the earliest times to
the founding of the Republic in 1960. This is the only such
book in English to treat the entire history of the island.
The first three chapters deal with ancient Cyprus. It should
be emphasized, however, that the author concentrates upon the
history of the island, not on the art or the archaeology.
Hence, the general reader or the visitor will not be able to
use this book as a guidebook to the major sites. B.

MYRON, R. and FANNING, R. The Putnam collegiate guide to the
    history of art, book 1. New York: G.P. Putnam's Sons 1966.
    Pp.206. $1.95 paper.

A useful outline of the history of art from Prehistoric cave
painting to Gothic sculpture and painting. This book is
designed as an aid for students. It is written in outline
form with each key idea underlined. At the end of each chapter
there are sample essay questions, and at the end of the entire
book there are multiple choice test questions. B.

ROBERTSON, D.S. Greek and Roman architecture, 2nd ed. New York:
   Cambridge Univ. Press 1969. Pp.407; 24 pls.; 135 ill. $3.95
   paper.

   First published in 1929.

   A handbook of the main trends in the history of Greek and
   Roman architecture from the earliest times to the founding of
   Constantinople. This book is especially valuable for English-
   speaking students since it synthesizes the works of many
   foreign scholars, including an informative chapter on Greek
   and Roman town-planning. Even though first published in 1929,
   this work is still useful as the only book that treats Greek
   and Roman architecture together in one volume. For discoveries
   since the second edition of 1943, especially those in the
   Athenian Agora and the Roman Forum, the reader will have to
   go to the individual excavation reports. The book contains
   copious plans and drawings, and at the end there is a valuable
   chronological table of Greek, Etruscan, and Roman buildings.   B.

RUSKIN, A. and BATTERBERRY, M. Greek and Roman art. (Discovering
   Art Series.) New York: McGraw-Hill 1968. Pp.192; 308 ill.
   $9.95 cloth.

   A readable account of the main developments in classical art,
   lavishly illustrated but lacking in architectural plans. This
   is a popular book designed to introduce the reader to ancient
   art; it is thus not recommended for class use. B/C.

II. THE AIMS, METHODS, AND HISTORY OF ARCHAEOLOGY.

The books in this area are generally excellent. There is no
one work which deals exclusively with the methods of Greek
and Roman archaeology. The paperback books in print concern
themselves mainly with the techniques of Prehistoric, Near
Eastern, or North American archaeology. But, as the techniques are the same in most cases, these books will also be
useful to the classical archaeologist.

BASS, G.F. Archaeology under water. Baltimore: Penguin 1970.
Pp.183; 62 pls.; 47 figs. $1.95 paper.

First published in 1966

For the hardback version of this book and a criticism of it,
see Section VII.

BROTHWELL, D. and P. Food in antiquity. (see Section VII.)

CERAM, C.W. Gods, graves, and scholars, 2nd rev. ed. New York:
Alfred A. Knopf 1967. Pp.441; 32 pls.; 4 maps. $8.95 cloth.

First published in 1949.

A popular account of the evolution and history of archaeology.
The author discusses the more spectacular discoveries of the
past two centuries and also concentrates on the characters of
the archaeologists involved; in fact, the book is almost a
series of miniature biographies. Part I deals with Pompeii,
Troy, Mycenae and Crete. The rest of the book is concerned

with Egyptian, Near Eastern and South American archaeology.
Because of its general nature, this book is only recommended
for the briefest of supplementary readings. B.

CERAM, C.W. The march of archaeology. New York: Alfred A. Knopf
1970. Pp.332; 8 pls.; 302 ill. $4.95 paper.

First published in 1957.

An excellent pictorial history of archaeology from the accidental
discovery in 1485 of a Roman sarcophagus containing the perfectly
preserved body of a young girl to the scientific methods of
the present day. The book is divided into five parts; the
first (68 pages in length), however, is the only one which
deals with Greek and Roman archaeology. The illustrations
are arranged in chronological order and are accompanied by an
explanatory text. This is the only such book of its kind in
English and makes a good companion to Gods, graves, and scholars.
B.

CHILDE, V.G. A short introduction to archaeology. New York:
Macmillan Co. 1962. Pp.127. $.95 paper.

First published in 1956.

A brief introduction (now a little out of date) to the
discipline of archaeology, treating such subjects as the
classification of data, archaeological sites and their
stratigraphy, and the interpretation of the finds. B.

CLARK, G. <u>Archaeology</u> <u>and</u> <u>society</u>, 3rd ed. rev. New York:
Barnes & Noble 1969. Pp.272; 52 ill. $2.50 paper.

First published in 1939.

An examination of the use of archaeology as a means of reconstructing the prehistory of Europe. The author describes how
prehistoric sites are found, what methods are used to excavate
them, how the finds are dated, and how archaeology helps us
to reconstruct the social, intellectual, and economic life
of the early Europeans. B.

DANIEL, G. <u>The</u> <u>origins</u> <u>and</u> <u>growth</u> <u>of</u> <u>archaeology</u>. Baltimore:
Penguin 1967. Pp.303; 7 pls. $1.65 paper.

A well-written and useful history of archaeology from the
earliest antiquarians and travellers to the modern systematic
techniques of excavation. There are liberal quotations from
the works of the early excavators; indeed, the book is really
an anthology of their writings. The author ends his work with
an account of the development of modern scientific methods. B.

DEETZ, J. <u>Invitation</u> <u>to</u> <u>archaeology</u>. New York: Natural History
Press 1967. Pp.150; 18 ill. $1.45 paper.

Although the author is primarily a North American archaeologist,
this book deals with all aspects of archaeology, exploring the
principles and methods of a modern excavator and provides a
good introduction to some of the scientific techniques
available. B.

-16-

GRINSELL, L., RAHTZ, P., and WARHURST, A. The preparation of
archaeological reports. New York: Humanities Press 1966. Pp.71;
5 ill. $2.00 cloth.

A useful handbook providing information about the technical aspects
of preparing an excavation report for publication. The authors
discuss the opportunities for publication, the preparation of text
and illustrations, the system of notes and references, and the
correcting of proofs. C.

KENYON, K. Beginning in archaeology, rev. ed. New York: Praeger 1966.
Pp.228; 11 pls.; 14 ill. $2.95 paper.

First published in 1952.

A general handbook for beginners in archaeology, covering the
geographical divisions within which archaeologists work and the
various ways in which one can become an archaeologist. The latter
part of the book is devoted to the technique of field work --
excavating, recording, dealing with finds, field surveys, and
air photography. B.

MEIGHAN, C.W. Archaeology: an introduction. San Francisco: Chandler
Publishing Co. 1966. Pp.197; 104 figs.; 8 tables. $4.95 paper.
A survey of the aims and methods of the archaeologist -- what he
studies and what he does. This book is valuable for its first
two chapters on the activities of the archaeologist, his tools,
and especially his methods of interpreting the data. Subsequent
chapters deal with specific excavations, such as the city of Ur,
the tomb of Tutankhamen, and several sites in the New World. B.

PAOR, L. de. Archaeology: an illustrated introduction. Baltimore:
Penguin 1967. Pp.111; 79 ill. $1.65 paper.
A general outline of the discipline of archaeology. The author
begins with a brief history of how archaeology developed. He
concentrates, however, on the methods of the excavator, paying
especial attention to the means by which a site is discovered,
the sorts of evidence which a site will produce, the classifying
of the finds, and the importance of stratigraphical evidence.
He closes with a brief chapter assessing the achievements of
modern archaeology. A.

PIGGOTT, S. Approach to archaeology. New York: McGraw-Hill 1965.
Pp.134; 8 pls.; 12 ill. $1.95 paper.

First published in 1959.

A non-technical introduction to the aims and techniques of the
excavator. Especially valuable are the last two chapters which
attempt to explain the difference in the methodologies of the
archaeologist, the prehistorian, and the historian. This book
is highly recommended for class use. A.

RACKL, H. W. Diving into the past. New York: Charles Scribner's
Sons 1968. Pp.292; 75 ill. $2.45 paper.

First published in 1964.

A popular account of archaeology under water from the early finds
by sponge divers to the discoveries of modern expeditions. The
author also discusses new technical advances in methods and
equipment. B.

RAPPORT, S. and WRIGHT, H. Archaeology. New York: Washington Square
Press 1964. Pp.367; 36 figs. $.90 paper.
An anthology of essays designed to provide a complete picture of

the discipline of archaeology. The editors have included discussions of archaeological problems, biographies of many of the more well-known excavators, and descriptions of famous discoveries. This book includes all periods and phases of archaeology from the Aegean to Asia and the New World. B.

REITH, A. Archaeological fakes. New York: Praeger 1970. Pp.183; 85 ill. $7.50 cloth.

First published in 1967.

An interesting survey of some of the more famous archaeological fakes. The author begins with a short history of art forgeries and then discusses specific examples, such as fakes in the fields of Palaeontology and Biology, forged Old Stone Age art, faked gold vessels, and false Runic inscriptions. He includes a brief chapter on the forgeries of Roman antiquities. B.

SHEPHERD, W. Archaeology. New York: The New American Library 1966. Pp.127; 18 pls.; 5 ill. $.60 paper.

A general account of what the archaeologist has learned about prehistoric man, his tools and weapons, and his homes and occupations. The author includes a chapter on the ancient civilizations of Egypt and Mesopotamia and devotes a whole section to the archaeology of America. Throughout the book, the emphasis is on how the archaeologist works, how he dates his finds, and how he relates them to one another. B.

WHEELER, MARGARET. History was buried: a source book of archaeology. New York: Hart Publishing Co. 1967. Pp.431; 133 ill. $3.95 paper.

A collection of excerpts from the writings of many excavators describing their discoveries. The author precedes each excerpt with a brief introduction. Included are essays on the Elgin marbles, Pompeii, and underwater discoveries. B.

WHEELER, MORTIMER. <u>Archaeology from the earth</u>. Baltimore: Penguin 1961. Pp.252; 24 pls.; 22 ill. $1.25 paper.

First published in 1954.

A critical survey of archaeological methods and techniques. This is an extremely detailed book and is thus recommended only as a teacher reference. C.

WOOLLEY, L. <u>Digging up the past</u>. Baltimore: Penguin 1954. Pp.142; 32 pls. $.95 paper.

First published in 1930.

A short outline of the methods of archaeology, including an interesting chapter on grave digging. Unfortunately, however, this book is now sadly out of date. C.

III. PREHISTORIC.

There is a wealth of material in this area. The books are of a
uniformly high quality; many of them can be used either as class
texts or for supplementary reading.

ALSOP, J.W. From the silent earth. New York: Harper and Row 1964.
Pp.296; 102 ill. $7.50 cloth.

A popular account primarily of the excavations at Pylos. The
author is a political reporter who uses his knowledge to interpret
the significance of the finds at Pylos and to examine the relationship
between Minoan Crete and mainland Greece. He introduces his
book with a brief account of the work of Schliemann at Troy and
Mycenae and that of Evans at Knossos. The first major section is
in the form of a brief history of Blegen's excavations at Pylos
with a description of the different parts of the palace. The
author, however, pays especial attention to the Linear B tablets
that were found and describes in detail the circumstances
surrounding their discovery and subsequently the work that went
into their decipherment. The second section ranges further
afield. The author discusses two of the major problems of Aegean
prehistory, the date of the fall of Knossos and that of the fall
of the Mycenaean world and the coming of the Dorians. In all,
this is one of the best popular books in the field of Greek
prehistory. Anecdote is cut to the minimum, and the author
presents the various theories and controversies in a very clear
and concise manner. He is interested primarily in the social
and economic history of the Aegean world, and the reader will

not find much on Minoan-Mycenaean art and architecture. The
photographs by Alison Frantz are excellent. This book is
highly recommended for supplementary reading. B.

BERNABO BREA, L. Sicily before the Greeks. (see section VII.)

BLEGEN, C.W. Troy and the Trojans. (see section VII.)

BLEGEN, C.W. and RAWSON, M. A guide to the palace of Nestor.
Cincinnati: University of Cincinnati Press 1962. Pp.32; 34 ill.
No price listed. Paper.
A general guide book to help visitors find their way around the
Palace of Nestor at Pylos. B.

BRANIGAN, K. The foundations of palatial Crete. New York: Praeger 1970.
Pp.232; 16 pls.; 47 figs. $9.50 cloth.
An excellent survey of Crete in the early Bronze Age from the
sub-Neolithic period to the building of the palaces in Middle
Minoan I. The author discusses the various aspects of early
Minoan civilization, its economy, religion, social organization,
domestic and funerary architecture, and art, but he concentrates
on a central theme: the debt of later palatial Crete to the early
Bronze Age. The section on early Minoan domestic architecture
is especially good. This is really the only such book in
English which concentrates on this period. At the back there is
a useful appendix of early Bronze Age sites which are open to
visitors. B.

BRAYMER, M. The walls of windy Troy. New York: Harcourt, Brace 1960.
Pp.189. $.60 paper.
A biography of Heinrich Schliemann, written especially for high
school students. B.

CHADWICK, J. The decipherment of Linear B, 2nd ed. New York:
Cambridge University Press 1970. Pp.164; 2 pls.; 17 figs.
$1.65 paper.

 First published in 1958.

An excellent general account of the history of Michael Ventris'
decipherment of Linear B. The author, Ventris' colleague, begins
with a brief discussion of the different scripts found by Evans
at Knossos, closing with a short description of Cypro-Minoan. He
then discusses the more important attempts at the decipherment of
Linear B up to 1950, after which he concentrates upon describing
the process by which Ventris made his decipherment in 1952.
Especially interesting are the two chapters entitled Growth
and Development and The Decipherment and the Critics. The former
gives the history and a summary of the first Ventris-Chadwick
article, "Evidence for Greek Dialect in the Mycenaean Archives,"
Journal of Hellenic Studies 73 (1953) 84-103. The latter discusses
the replies of various critics to this article and gives a
synopsis of the subsequent Ventris-Chadwick book, Documents in
Mycenaean Greek (Cambridge 1956). The author concludes his
work with a chapter on life in Mycenaean Greece as deduced from
the deciphered Linear B texts. At the end he has added a
postscript which takes into account the developments since the
original edition of 1958. B.

COTTRELL, L. The bull of Minos. New York: Grosset and Dunlap 1962.
Pp.234; 50 ill. $2.50 paper.

 First published in 1953.

A popular account of the discoveries at Troy and Knossos. The
author weaves his story around the lives and quests of Heinrich
Schliemann and Sir Arthur Evans. Because of its popular nature,
this book is not recommended for class use. C.

FINLEY, M. I. Early Greece: the bronze and archaic ages. (Ancient
  Cultures and Society Series.) New York: Norton and Co. 1970.
  Pp.155; 4 figs.; 4 pls.; 6 maps. $1.65 paper.
  The first part of this book contains a good cultural history
  of the Aegean in the bronze age. The author includes an
  interesting chapter on Cyprus and the Cyclades, an area which is
  often omitted in surveys of this kind. One only wishes that this
  chapter were longer. The second part on the archaic age is
  not as good. It is far too sketchy; for instance, in talking
  about the burial practices of the Dark Ages, the author mentions
  changes in the grave structure, but he nowhere tells us what
  these changes were nor how the structures differed from those
  of previous ages. Again, the social and political history of
  Athens in the Archaic period is dismissed in ten pages and that
  of Sparta in eleven. Despite the above reservations, however,
  students may find this book valuable for its chapters on the
  Bronze Age. B.

FINLEY, M. I. The world of Odysseus, rev. ed. New York: Viking Press
  1965. Pp.176. $1.25 paper.
      First published in 1954.
  A well-written account of the society in which Homer conceived his
  heroes to live. The author discusses such topics as wealth and
  labor, household, kin, and community, and morals and values.

This book is a social history of the Homeric world and not an
archaeological treatment. It thus contains no plans or
photographs. A.

FORSDYKE, J. Greece before Homer. New York: Norton and Co. 1964.
Pp.176; 8 ill. $1.55 paper.

An examination of how mythology can be used to piece together
the early history of Greece and of how prehistoric narratives
were adopted in historical Greek literature. Since this book
is now out of date, it is not recommended either for class use
or for supplementary reading. C.

GRAHAM, J.W. The palaces of Crete. Princeton: Princeton University
Press 1969. Pp.269; 154 ill. $4.95 paper.

First published in 1962.

An excellent and comprehensive review of Minoan palace architecture,
concentrating upon three major palaces: Knossos, Phaistos, and
Mallia. The author, however, does not neglect the domestic
architecture and includes a chapter on the minor palaces, villas,
and houses. He attempts, by a comparison of similar features,
to determine what is typical of Minoan architecture. For example,
on the basis of its architectural elements, he is able to
identify the building at Nirou Khani about eight miles east of
Herakleion as a private house, thereby correcting the earlier
identifications of Evans and the Greek excavator, Xanthoudides,
that it was the headquarters of a High Priest. Especially
interesting are the chapters on building materials and forms,
furnishings, and the procedures and principles of Minoan
architecture. For the paperback edition, the author has added
an addendum to the preface in which he discusses very briefly

the newly discovered palace at Kato Zakro. The book contains
good photographs and copious plans and reconstructions. B.

HIGGINS, R. Minoan and Mycenaean art. New York: Praeger 1967.
Pp.216; 241 ill. $3.95 paper.

An excellent general survey of bronze age art and architecture
in the Aegean. Unfortunately, this book is not evenly balanced
in all fields. The concentration appears to be on the
decorated pottery, the frescoes, and the jewellery to the
exclusion of the architecture. At times this can be confusing.
For instance, the author discusses the seal impressions found
in the House of Tiles at Lerna but dismisses in one sentence
the architecture of the house and, indeed, that of the entire
site. Similarly, he includes a discussion of several frescoes
found at Tiryns, but nowhere treats the architecture of the
palace in which they were found. In spite of the above reservations,
however, this book is recommended for use as a class text. A.

HOOD, S. The home of the heroes: the Aegean before the Greeks.
New York: McGraw-Hill 1967. Pp.144; 122 ill. $2.95 paper.
The author presents a general survey of Aegean prehistory,
focusing on such problems as the origins of the Greek people
and of the Greek language. He is primarily interested in Minoan
Crete and indeed devotes the majority of his book to this area.
Mycenaean Greece is thus dismissed in a chapter of twenty-two
pages. The illustrations are excellent, especially the ones
in color. B.

HOOD, S. The Minoans. (see section VII.)

HUTCHINSON, R.W. <u>Prehistoric</u> <u>Crete</u>. Baltimore: Penguin 1962.
Pp.373; 32 ill. $2.25 paper.

The author traces the development of Minoan civilization period
by period and discusses the archaeological remains. He gives
an account of the material culture and develops a picture of the
nature of Minoan society. The concluding chapter, however, on
Geometric and Orientalizing Crete is far too incomplete. For
instance, the sections on Lato and Prinias are sketchy. The
author simply mentions the architectural sculptures from Prinias
but nowhere explains their significance. Similarly, he discusses
the Daedalic style of the Orientalizing period but does not
include photographs or drawings to illustrate his text. Although
this book is comprehensive for the Minoan period, its organization
is confusing, and thus for students it may be hard to read. C.

McDONALD, W.A. <u>Progress</u> <u>into</u> <u>the</u> <u>past</u>. Bloomington: Indiana
University Press 1969. Pp.476; 101 ill. $4.95 paper.

First published in 1967.

A biographical and historical account of the rediscovery of
Mycenaean civilization. The author reviews the evidence as
it has been accumulating over the past century and pays
especial attention to the lives and works of three of the most
famous excavators: Schliemann. Evans, and Blegen. This is an
excellent survey of all aspects of the Mycenaean world and is
highly recommended for supplementary reading. B.

MATZ, F. <u>The</u> <u>art</u> <u>of</u> <u>Crete</u> <u>and</u> <u>early</u> <u>Greece</u>. (Art of the World.)
New York: Crown Publishers 1965. Pp.259; 56 pls.; 22 ill.
$6.95 cloth.

An excellent and balanced survey of Minoan and Mycenaean art
and architecture. One minor criticism is that the author
might have devoted more space to the culture and major sites
of the Middle Helladic period - a period which has often been
sadly neglected in surveys and handbooks. This book is
especially good for its color plates and is highly recommended
for use as a class text. A.

MAVOR, J.W. Voyage to Atlantis. New York: G.P. Putnam's Sons 1969.
Pp.320; 32 pls.; 40 ill. $6.95 cloth.
The author presents a popular account of his two expeditions to
the island of Thera. He discusses in general terms what
discoveries were made to verify the theory that Thera is the
site of Atlantis. For the archaeologically minded reader,
there are supplementary appendices with charts. B.

MELLERSH, H.E.L. Minoan Crete. (Life in Ancient Lands.) New York:
G.P. Putnam's Sons 1967. Pp.143; 14 pls.; 72 ill. $5.95 cloth.
Another popular work on the civilization of the Minoans. The
author concentrates on delineating a picture of the life and
thoughts of the people. One caveat, however, must be kept in
mind. He discussse the major Cretan palaces but in the majority
of cases fails to accompany his text with architectural plans,
thus causing the reader some confusion. Indeed, the only plan
that is provided is one of the palace at Knossos. Otherwise,
the book is clearly written; students may find it useful for
providing a general background to the archaeology of Crete. B.

MYLONAS, G.E. Mycenae's last century of greatness. Sydney:
International Scholarly Book Service 1968. Pp.39; 20 ill.
$3.00 paper.

An account of the investigation of the so-called "House of
Columns" at Mycenae. The author shows that the building is
not a house but the center of the east wing of the palace and
that it was built in the second half of the Thirteenth Century
B.C. C.

NILSSON, M.P. The Mycenaean origin of Greek mythology. New York:
Norton and Co. 1962. Pp.258. $1.55 paper.

First published in 1932.

An attempt to find a Mycenaean background for many of the stories
of Greek mythology. The author discusses such topics as the age
of Greek mythology, Mycenaean centers and mythological centers,
Herakles, and Olympos. C.

PAGE, D.L. History and the Homeric Iliad. (Sather Classical
Lectures 31.) Berkeley: University of California Press 1963.
Pp.350; i4 ill. $1.95 paper.

First published in 1959.

An examination of the Iliad based not only on archaeological
discoveries but also on a close analysis of the text. The
author discusses the history of Troy and the historical
background to the Trojan war as well as the authorship of
the poem. The first chapter provides an important discussion of
what is known about the relations between the Hittites and the
Greeks. B.

PALMER, L.R. <u>Mycenaeans</u> <u>and</u> <u>Minoans</u>, 2nd ed. rev. New York:
Alfred A. Knopf 1965. Pp.368; 20 pls.; 49 ill. $7.95 cloth.
An interpretation of the evidence presented by the Linear B
tablets and what they show about Mycenaean society. In Part I
the author first gives a brief history of Ventris' decipherment
of Linear B and then discusses the tablets from Pylos. He has,
however, rewritten Part II for the revised edition. In this
second part, he examines not only the Linear B tablets from
Knossos but also many of the field notebooks of Evans and his
assistant, Duncan Mackenzie, and shows that there are discrepancies
between the field records and the final conclusions of the
excavators. Accordingly, he proposes a new chronology for the
tablets, dating them to the last "reoccupation" phase of the
palace around 1200 B.C. B.

PALMER, L.R. <u>A</u> <u>new</u> <u>guide</u> <u>to</u> <u>the</u> <u>palace</u> <u>at</u> <u>Knossos</u>. New York:
Praeger 1969. Pp.144; 6 pls.; 23 ill.; 4 plans. $6.50 cloth.
A new work on the palace at Knossos, claiming to correct many
of the errors in Evans' <u>Palace</u> <u>of</u> <u>Minos</u>. This book is primarily
a guide book to the palace. The author takes the visitor
through the palace quarter by quarter, and at each significant
place he interprets the excavation results, as dervied from
the new evidence. Emphasis has been placed on famous works of
Minoan art, since these are of interest to the visitor. An
appendix describes the knossos exhibits in the Archaeological
Museum at Herakleion. B.

PAYNE, R. The gold of Troy. New York: Paperback Library, Inc.
1961. Pp.224. $.75 paper.

First published in 1959.

A biography of Heinrich Schliemann designed for the general
reader. Unfortunately, the author misleads the reader by
presenting Schliemann's excavations at Troy and Mycenae as a
treasure hunt -- this was far from being the case. C.

PENDLEBURY, J.D.S. The archaeology of Crete. New York: Norton
and Co. 1965. Pp.400; 43 pls.; 53 ill. $2.75 paper.

First published in 1939.

An important survey of the culture of Crete from the Neolithic
period down to Roman times. This book not only summarizes
Evans' work but also draws together information that had
accumulated since 1900 from sites all over the island. The
author follows the chronological approach and includes valuable
lists of sites for each period. Even though this book is now
out of date, it is still important as the first real synthesis
of evidence from settlements throughout the whole island. C.

PIGGOTT, S. Ancient Europe: a survey. Chicago: Aldine Publishing
Co. 1965. Pp.340; 143 figs.; 51 pls. $3.95 paper.

A survey of prehistoric Europe from the beginnings of agriculture
to classical antiquity. This excellent book begins at a date
somewhat before 6000 B.C. and ends with the incorporation of
much of the Europaean world into the Roman empire. The text
is clearly organized with good plans and photographs. For the
student of archaeology, there are copious notes at the end of
each chapter and a rather extensive select bibliography. B.

SAMUEL, A.E. The Mycenaeans in history. Englewood Cliffs, N.J.:
   Prentice-Hall 1966. Pp.158; 49 ill.; 5 maps. $2.45 paper.
   An historical approach to Mycenaean civilization. The author
   attempts to find out what early Greek society was like and how
   it grew and declined. B.
TAYLOUR, W.D. The Mycenaeans. (see section VII.)
VERMEULE, E. Greece in the bronze age. Chicago: University of
   Chicago Press 1972. Pp.406; 48 pls.; 52 ill. $3.95 paper.
   First published in 1964.
A comprehensive survey of prehistoric Greece from the Stone Age
to the fall of the Mycenaean palaces in the Thirteenth Century B.C.
The author discusses such topics as the Early and Middle Bronze
Ages, the shaft graves, and the society and history of the
period. At the end, there is a useful chart of representative
pottery types, followed by an appendix on crops and food. A
short preface of three pages, primarily bibliographical in
nature, takes into account the discoveries since the original
hardback edition of 1964. The student, however, may find this
book a little confusing, since it includes few architectural
plans or reconstructions. C.
WEBSTER, T.B.L. From Mycenae to Homer, 2nd ed. New York: Norton
   and Co. 1964. Pp.333; 38 ill. $1.85 paper.
   First published in 1958.
A unique and comprehensive study of Greek art and poetry in the
Mycenaean, sub-Mycenaean, and Geometric periods. Especially
interesting is the chapter on Mycenaean pottery, in which the

author suggests that, because of the amount of Mycenaean pottery found at Troy, there might have been a Mycenaean trading post in Troy VIIA, as there apparently was at Ugarit and elsewhere, and that it also was a member of the circle of Mycenaean kingdoms. B.

IV. ARCHAIC, CLASSICAL, HELLENISTIC.

The heaviest concentration of paperbacks and hardbacks occurs
here. The entire range of subject-matter is covered, including
several good archaeological guide books. Two areas, however,
are neglected; what are needed are paperbacks dealing exclusively
with Hellenistic art and archaeology and with the art of Sicily
and Southern Italy.

AKURGAL, E. The art of Greece: its origins in the Mediterranean and
Near East (Art of the World.) New York: Crown Publishers 1968.
Pp.258; 68 pls.; 171 ill. $6.95 cloth.

The author divides this book into two parts -- in the first,
Assyrian, Babylonian, Aramaean, Neo-Hittite, and Phoenician
art is systematically analyzed; in the second, the relation
between early Greek art and that of the civilizations of the
Near East is examined. One caveat, however, must be kept in
mind. In Part I, the author devotes considerable attention
to Neo-Hittite architecture (26 pages), but he does not follow
this through in Part II by discussing the Eastern influences
on Greek Geometric and Orientalizing architecture. Indeed, he
dismisses early Greek architecture in a page and a half. He
also neglects to discuss the early art of Cyprus, thereby
failing to recognize the importance of this island as a half-
way point between the Near East and Greece. Otherwise, this is
an excellent and unusual book, extremely well illustrated. B.

BALDRY, H.C. Ancient Greek literature in its living context.
New York: McGraw-Hill 1968. Pp.144; 123 ill. $2.95 paper.

An examination of the archaeological and artistic background to
Greek literature. The author discusses sculpture, vase painting,
and architecture in relation to its literary background and shows
how archaeology can broaden our understanding of Greek literature.
A major criticism, however, is the rather sketchy treatment
the author gives to the Greek theater. For example, he describes
the various parts of the theater but nowhere provides a plan
of any Greek theater nor discusses the problems of staging a
Greek drama. This book is well illustrated. A/B.

BARRON, J. Greek sculpture. New York: E.P. Dutton and Co. 1965.
Pp.160; 157 ill. $1.95 paper.

A pictorial survey of Greek sculpture. The accompanying text
is adequate, but quite weak in Hellenistic sculpture. For
instance, the author does not discuss the important developments
in portraiture nor does he take into account the neo-classicizing
movement of the Second and First Centuries B.C. and the copying
school which developed under Pasiteles. There is much more to
Hellenistic sculpture than the standard pieces, such as the Venus
de Milo and the Victory of Samothrace, usually included in
handbooks. B.

BEAN, G.E. Aegean Turkey: an archaeological guide. New York:
Praeger 1966. Pp.288; 75 pls.; 53 ill. $8.95 cloth.
An excellent guide book to the archaeological sites (both Greek
and Roman) on Turkey's Aegean coast. The area covered is
roughly that which is in comfortable reach from Smyrna, excluding,
however, sites south of Miletus and Didyma. This book is written

especially for those who wish to travel in western Turkey.
The archaeological description of each site is prefaced by an
historical introduction, and there are copious plans. To
present a complete picture of the area, the author also includes
a few sites that have little to show in the way of tangible
ruins. This book can also be used profitably as supplementary
reading for course work. B.

BEAN, G.E. Turkey beyond the Maeander: an archaeological guide.
Totowa, N.J.: Rowman and Littlefield 1971. Pp.267; 78 pls.;
47 ill.; 1 map. $11.50 cloth.
This book has the same format and method of presentation as the
author's Aegean Turkey. It deals with the area that lies to the
south of that covered in the earlier book and which corresponds
with the ancient Caria. B.

BEAN, G.E. Turkey's southern shore: an archaeological guide.
New York: Praeger 1968. Pp.188; 77 pls.; 30 ill. $7.95 cloth.
An excellent companion work to the author's Aegean Turkey
and Turkey beyond the Maeander. This book follows the same
method of presentation and covers the area of the southern
coast of Turkey, roughly equivalent to the ancient Pamphylia. B.

BEAZLEY, J.D. and ASHMOLE, B. Greek sculpture and painting.
New York: Cambridge University Press 1966. Pp.111; 248 ill.
$7.50 cloth.
   First published in 1932.
A survey of Greek sculpture and painting to the end of the
Hellenistic period. Unfortunately, the reprint of 1966 does not
alter the original text published in 1932. All that the authors

have done to take into account the discoveries of the past
forty years is to add an inadequate two page appendix at the
back and to update the bibliography. The gaps are especially
felt in the area of Hellenistic painting and mosaics. For
instance, the tomb panels from Kazanlak and Paestum, the painted
stelai from Pagasae, and the Centuripe vases present important
evidence for Hellenistic painting but are here omitted.
Similarly, the authors include such famous works as the Alexander
mosaic and the Dioskourides mosaic from Pompeii, but do not
mention the mosaics from Olynthus and Pella. Indeed, in general
the concentration of the text appears to be on Greek sculpture,
and in this respect it is excellent, although the short paragraph
in the appendix on the Daedalic style of early monumental
sculpture needs to be expanded to include a thorough discussion
of this phase of Greek plastic art. If the above reservations
are kept in mind, students may find this book useful for
supplementary reading. B.

BLUEMEL, C. Greek sculptors at work. New York: Praeger 1970.
   Pp.85; 67 ill. $8.95 cloth.

   First published in 1927; first English ed. 1955.
An excellent survey of the technical methods of Greek sculptors.
The author discusses the various tools used, the successive
stages of work, and the different periods of development. There
are copious illustrations, many of which are not found in the
usual handbooks. B.

BOARDMAN, J. Athenian black figure vases. New York: Oxford University
Press 1974. 388 ill. $10.00 cloth.

An excellent survey of the history of Attic black figure vase
painting, covering the various artists, styles, mythological
subjects, and decorative motifs. B.

BOARDMAN, J. Greek art. New York: Praeger 1964. Pp.286; 251 ill.
$3.95 paper.

A concise hsitory of Greek art and architecture from Geometric
times to the end of the First Century B.C. The author is at
his best when he discusses the Geometric, Orientalizing, and
Archaic periods, although by emphasizing the vase painting and
clay and bronze figurines of these periods he overlooks the
important area of architecture. Geometric architecture, especially,
receives sketchy treatment. Much important evidence for the
building activity of the Geometric people has come to light in
the past two decades, and we have a considerable number of
examples of both domestic and religious buildings. There are,
for instance, the oval houses at Athens and Old Smyrna, the
rectangular ones at Andros and Emporio, and the temple remains
at Dreros, Perachora, and Eretria. For the orientalizing period,
there is the temple at Neandria and that at Prinias with its
important architectural sculptures. These buildings illustrate
how the early Greeks lived and worshipped and a discussion of
them should be included in every handbook of Greek art. A
second criticism of this book concerns the author's treatment
of the Fourth Century B.C. In this important period, which is
really a prelude to the Hellenistic age, a number of changes

were made in both architectural and sculptural concepts. The
author, however, does not discuss these changes in any organized
fashion. For instance, he fails to note the decline of the
Doric order, the increased use of the Corinthian one, and the
trend away from religious architecture to more elaborate
domestic and political buildings. Similarly, for the sculpture
of the period, he does not treat systematically the works of
Scopas, Praxiteles, and Lysippus, and fails to emphasize the
changes in the style and concept of their works from the plastic
art of the Fifth Century B.C. Despite the above reservations,
however, this book can be used successfully as a text for a
beginning survey of Greek art. It is well illustrated. A.

BOARDMAN, J. The Greeks overseas. Baltimore: Penguin 1964. Pp.288;
24 pls.; 75 ill. $1.45 paper.

A well written account of the material evidence for the early
relations between the Greeks and their neighbors. This book
deals primarily with the archaeological evidence for the Greeks
in the Near East, Egypt, Italy and Sicily, and in the Black
Sea region. The author also discusses the effect of the Greeks
upon native populations and the effect of the natives on the
Greeks. Especially interesting is the chapter entitled Italy,
Sicily, and the West, in which, after a brief introduction, he
treats each Greek colony individually. Two major omissions,
however, occur. First, there is no discussion of the problems
which occur in the chronology of the foundation dates of these
colonies, and second, there is no mention of the excavations at

Morgantina and the evidence which this city presents for the
extent of the Greek penetration to the center of the island. B.
BOARDMAN, J. Pre-classical. Baltimore: Penguin 1967. Pp.186;
104 ill. $2.95 paper.
An excellent introduction to Greek art from Minoan Crete to
the end of the Archaic era. The author begins each period
with a brief sketch of the society before he examines the
development of the art. This book is especially good for
the Geometric and Archaic periods, but the same criticisms
which were made against the author's Greek art also apply
here. Vase painting and the minor arts are emphasized at the
expense of architecture. (This is felt especially in the
chapter on Minoans and Mycenaeans in which not a single
building is discussed.) Despite this major omission, however,
the book is still the best paperback which treats the Geometric
and Archaic periods. It is well organized and easy to read
and is thus recommended for use as a class text. A.
BRADFORD, E. Ulysses found. New York: Harcourt, Brace & Co. 1968.
Pp.238; 13 pls.; 6 maps. $1.65 paper.
     First published in 1964.
An attempt to trace Odysseus' wanderings on his way home from
Troy. The author is a sailor who spent three years in the
Mediterranean trying to identify the places mentioned in the
Odyssey. As a result he has been able to recreate, in terms
intelligible to the general reader, the course of Odysseus'
journey. B.

BRUNO, V.J., ed. The Parthenon. (Norton Critical Studies in Art
History.) New York: Norton and Co. 1974. Pp.334; 67 ill.;
63 pls. $4.95 paper.

A collection of essays by various scholars on the art, architecture,
and history of the Parthenon. The essays have been carefully
selected, and, taken together, they present a thorough picture
of the Parthenon. One drawback to this book is that the plates
have been badly reproduced and are not as clear or sharp as
they might have been. This is often the case when plates are
reproduced from their original printings. B.

BULLITT, O.H. The search for Sybaris. Philadelphia: J.B. Lippincott
Co. 1969. Pp.238; 22 ill. $6.95 cloth.

A good popular account of the eight year search for the Greek city
of Sybaris in Southern Italy. The author begins with a brief
history of early Greek civilization and then gives a short
account of the history of Sybaris and her neighbors. Especially
interesting is his discussion of prior expeditions to find the
city and his account of the expedition conducted by the Museum
of the University of Pennsylvania. B.

BURN, A.R. The warring states of Greece: from their rise to the
Roman conquest. New York: McGraw Hill 1968. Pp.144; 136 ill.
$2.95 paper.

An excellent brief archaeological and historical account of
the various Greek city ststes until the Roman conquest. The
author pays especial attention to the cultural and artistic
attainments of the cities he discusses. One weakness is that

when talking about historical events he neglects to mention
the ancient authors who describe these events. For instance,
in discussing the reforms of Solon he nowhere states that one
of the most important sources for these reforms is Solon's own
poetry. This book, however, can be used as a text for a
beginning course in Greek civilization. It is well
illustrated. A.

CARPENTER, R. The architects of the Parthenon. Baltimore: Penguin
1970. Pp.193; 75 ill. $2.65 paper.

An important book on the architecture of the Parthenon. The
author challenges the present idea that the Parthenon was built
with extreme care and precision and shows that there was a great
deal of makeshift involved. He also suggests that the two
architects, Ictinus and Callicrates, were not collaborators
but rivals. Other temples of the period are also discussed in
this book which contains useful plans and excellent photographs.
B.

CARPENTER, R. The esthetic basis of Greek art, rev. ed. Bloomington:
Indiana University Press 1959. Pp.177; 8 ill. $1.75 paper.

First published in 1921.

An interesting book which examines Greek artistic procedure in
order to arrive at some fundamental esthetic principles. The
author discusses the esthetics not only of Greek sculpture but
also of Greek architecture. Unfortunately, since the argumentation
is difficult to follow, this book is not recommended as a
textbook. C.

CARPENTER, R. Greek sculpture. Chicago: University of Chicago
Press 1971. Pp.274; 47 pls.; 3 ill. $3.95 paper.

First published in 1960.

A discussion of the technical laws which governed the development
of Greek sculpture. The author does not write a history of the
individual artists and their works, but he examines the evolution
of the different sculptural styles and of the technical procedures
involved. This book is heavy on the philosophy of esthetics,
and students may find it most difficult to follow the argumentation.
It is thus not recommended as a textbook. C.

CHAMOUX, F. Ancient Greek sculpture from the museums of Athens.
New York: The New American Library 1968. Pp.56; 32 ill.
$1.25 paper.

A brief pictorial survey of Greek sculpture. The illustrative
examples are taken from the most important works in the various
museums at Athens. The thirty-two color plates of this book
are preceded by a short introduction of twenty pages, in which
each of the examples is placed in its proper artistic and
historical perspective. B.

COOK, J.M. The Greeks in Ionia and the east. (see section VII.)

COOK, R.M. Greek art: its development, character, and influence.
New York: Farrar, Straus, and Giroux 1973. Pp.277; 96 pls.
$4.95 paper.

An excellent and comprehensive treatment of all aspects of Greek
art and architecture. The author divides his subject into eight
sections, each comprising one area of Greek art, such as painted
pottery, panel and mural painting, sculpture, metalwork, gems

and coins, and architecture. He treats each subject chronologically.
What makes this book especially valuable is that he does not
ignore the Hellenistic period but gives a full account of the
various developments in this era. This book can be used either
as a text or for supplementary reading for any course in Greek art
and architecture. A/B.

COOK, R.M. The Greeks until Alexander. (see section VII.)

COOK, R. and KATHLEEN. Southern Greece: an archaeological guide.
New York: Praeger 1968. Pp.217; 15 ill.; 31 plans. $6.95 cloth.
A guide book of Attica, Delphi, and the Peloponnese for the
archaeologically minded traveller. The chief fault is that at
times the traveller is forgotten in favor of heavy archaeological
material. For example, the authors take him to such relatively
inaccessible places as the Corycian cave above Delphi, the
Sanctuary of Despoina at Lycosura, and the ash altar of Zeus
on top of Mt. Lykaion but fail to point out their significance
or why he should make the effort to visit them. This book is
best used in conjunction with the Blue Guide to Greece, which
gives practical information about restaurants, hotels, and
museums and distinguishes between the important sites and those
with very little to show for themselves. B.

DEVAMBEZ, P. Greek painting. (Compass History of Art I.) New York:
Viking Press 1962. Pp.212; 176 ill. $2.25 paper.
A pictorial history of Greek painting. The majority of this
book is made up of plates, many of them in color, illustrating
the development of Greek painting. Several examples, such as two
orientalizing vases from Crete and an Attic white-ground alabastron,

are unusual in that they do not appear in the standard handbboks.
At the beginning there is an introduction of thirty-six pages.
There are two drawbacks to this book. The first is that the
examples which the author discusses in his introduction are not
cross-referenced with the appropriate plates at the back, thus
causing the reader great confusion, and the second is that the
plates illustrating Hellenistic painting are far too few. There
are only three examples of Italiote vase painting from the
various schools of the Fourth Century B.C. and no representations
of the polychromatic style from the Lipari Islands and Centuripe.
Similarly, the pebble mosaics of Olynthus and Pella are largely
neglected. The author does include an illustration of one of
the huntsmen from the "Lion Hunt" mosaic from Pella, but it
would have made more sense to have included a picture of the
entire mosaic rather than a small segment of it. Furthermore,
he dates this particular mosaic to ca. 410 B.C. but in the
introduction gives no reasons for this radical departure from
the traditional dating to the last third of the Fourth
Century B.C.   B/C.

EXCAVATIONS of the Athenian Agora: picture books. Princeton:
American School of Classical Studies. Pp.32. Paper.

No.1.   Pots and pans of classical Athens. (1959) $.50.

No.2.   The stoa of Attalos II in Athens. (1959) $.50.

No.3.   Miniature sculpture from the Athenian agora (1959) $.50.

No.4.   The Athenian citizen. (1960) $.50.

No.5.   Ancient portraits from the Athenian agora. (1960) $.50.

No.6.   Amphoras and the ancient wine trade. (1961) $.50.

No.7.   The middle ages in the Athenian agora. (1961) $.50.

No.8.   Garden lore of ancient Athens. (1963) $1.00.

No.9.   Lamps from the Athenian agora. (1964) $.50.

No.10. Inscriptions from the Athenian agora. (1966) $.50.

No.11. Waterworks from the Athenian agora. (1968) $.50.

No.12. An ancient shopping center: the Athenian agora. (1971) $.70.

No.13. Early burials from the agora cemeteries. (1973) $.70.

A series of small picture books illustrating certain aspects of
the Agora excavations. The general reader and the student will
find these interesting because they present a clear picture
of the political, economic, and private life in ancient Athens. B.

FAIRBANKS, A. Greek art: the basis of later European art.
(Our debt to Greece and Rome series.) New York: Cooper Square
1963. Pp.136; 16 pls.; 5 ill. $3.50 cloth.

A short book dealing with the esthetics of Greek art. The author
first discusses the unique appeal of Greek art to the modern
mind and then passes on to an analysis of what is meant by the
classical tradition. He ends with an attempt to define the
Greek spirit and to see how it manifests itself in later European
art. This is a sketchy and inconclusive book; the plates at
the end have been badly reproduced. C.

GUIDO, M. Sicily: an archaeological guide. New York: Praeger 1967.
Pp.219; 36 ill. $6.95 cloth.

A superb guide book to Sicily for the archaeologically minder
traveller, spanning the Prehistoric, Greek, and Roman ruins.

There are copious plans of the various archaeological sites and
museums. One exception is that the author, while presenting an
historical introduction to the important city of Morgantina,
does not provide a plan of the city nor a description of its
major monuments. She does give, however, plenty of practical
information on bus tours, hotels, and museums, with adequate
directions of how to reach the places of interest if one is
travelling by car. B.

GUIDO, M. Southern Italy: an archaeological guide. Park Ridge, N.J.:
The Noyes Press 1973. Pp.222; 31 pls.; 33 ill. $10.00 cloth.
A companion work to the author's guide to Sicily, this book
describes the Prehistoric, Greek, and Roman sites of Southern
Italy (Magna Graecia). The book is divided into six chapters,
each one consisting of an area traversed by a major road.
Within each chapter the sites are arranged in alphabetical
order. This is the first such guide of its kind; it concentrates
on a description of the monuments and of the material located
in the various museums. The reader will not find here general
tourist information. The author describes in detail, but yet
in terms intelligible to the general reader, both the well-known
towns, such as Pompeii and Herculaneum, and the lesser known
sites, such as Egnazia and Velia, hitherto chiefly described in
Italian archaeological periodicals. Mrs. Guido devotes
considerable space to the description of the contents of the
various museums, often providing detailed floor plans to
accompany these descriptions. A major omission, however,

must be noted. The author does not describe the Greco-Roman ruins in Naples (Neapolis) and Taranto (Tarentum). These are difficult to find and are obscured by the modern towns. A description of how to find these scattered ruins and their importance would be useful. Copious maps, plans, and charts. B.

HAFNER, G. The art of Crete, Mycenae, and Greece. New York: Harry Abrams 1968. Pp.264; 267 ill. $7.95 cloth.

Primarily a pictorial history of Greek art and architecture from Minoan times to the First Century B.C. There is a brief general introduction of seven pages. The rest of the book consists of illustrations, under each of which the author places a brief description and makes comments about identification and style. As is so common in books of this kind, the author concentrates on sculpture and painting but sadly neglects architecture. The major attraction of this book are the 140 color plates. B.

HOLLOWAY, R.R. A view of Greek art. New York: Harper and Row 1974. Pp.213; 151 ill.; 5 maps. $4.95 paper.

An excellent survey of monumental Greek art. The author does not write a chronological history of Greek art but seeks to answer the questions of why Greek art developed in the way it did. Consequently, he concentrates on the archaic period and devotes little space to the Fourth Century B.C. and to the Hellenistic period. The text is clearly written. A good feature is that wide margins have been left on the right and left sides of the pages. These contain references to books and articles (primarily in

English) which the student can consult for further reading.
Used together with Pollitt's Art and Experience in Classical
Greece (see below), it can form the nucleus (as a class text)
for any undergraduate course in Greek art and architecture. A.
HOMANN-WEDEKING, H. The art of archaic Greece. (Art of the World.)
New York: Crown Publishers 1968. Pp.224; 54 pls.; 37 ill.
$6.95 cloth.

A survey of the early art and architecture in Greece from 1050 B.C.
to the end of the archaic period. The author discusses this art
in terms of its political, cultural, and economic settings. The
same general criticism applies to this book as it does to
Boardman's Greek art and Pre-classical, namely, the lack of
space devoted to the increasingly important area of Geometric
architecture. The text has been translated from the German; at
times the translation is awkward and the syntax hard to follow
and may cause the student some confusion. The illustrations,
however, are excellent. B.

HOYLE, P. Delphi. New York: Fernhill House 1967. Pp.194; 42 ill.
$6.50 cloth.

An enthusiastic account of the archaeology and history of Delphi
written in terms intelligible to the general reader. The author
discusses the religious life of the sanctuary, the various
festivals, the mechanics involved in seeking an oracle, and some
of the more famous oracular responses. He also describes the
buildings in the sanctuary and ends his book with an account of the
attempt by the Greek poet Anghelos Sikelianos and his wife to

produce the first modern festival at Delphi in 1927. B.

MacKENDRICK, P. The Greek stones speak. New York: The New American

    Library 1966. Pp.430; 175 ill. $.95 paper.

      First published in 1962.

    A well written and clear account of the story of archaeology in

    Greek lands. The author's purpose is twofold: to write a cultural

    history based upon the material remains uncovered by the archaeologists

    and to show how the archaeologist uses his evidence. Special

    attention is paid to architecture and the development of

    architectural forms. This book is highly recommended for

    students. A.

MARTIN, R. Living architecture: Greek. New York: Grosset and

    Dunlap 1968. Pp.192; 84 pls.; 17 plans. $7.95 cloth.

    This book does not concern itself so much with the Greek temple

    (as do the majority of handbooks) as with lesser known monuments,

    such as private houses, stoas, gates, and fortifications. The

    author devotes much space to the materials of construction,

    roofing, ceilings, lighting, costs, and the provision of the

    materials. He ends with a chapter on the principles of architectural

    composition. The one drawback of this book is its haphazard

    organization. There is no attempt to cross-reference the plates

    with the text, thus causing the reader much confusion. B/C.

MINGAZZINI, P. Greek pottery painting. (Cameo Series.) New York:

    Tudor Publishing Co. 1969. Pp.157; 69 pls. $2.95 cloth.

    A short survey of Greek vase painting. Each of the sixty-nine

    color plates has a brief paragraph of identification and

description attached to it. The majority of the examples are
the standard ones usually found in popular works of this kind.
Several, however, are unfamiliar and appear here for the first
time in color. A useful explanatory text is interspersed
throughout the plates, and the specific examples discussed are
cross-referenced with the appropriate illustrations. B.

MYLONAS, G.E. Eleusis and the Eleusinian mysteries. Princeton:
Princeton University Press 1969. Pp.346; 88 ill. $4.95 paper.
First published in 1961.

A thorough survey of the archaeology, history, legends, and
religion of the Sanctuary of Demeter at Eleusis. Especially
interesting is the third chapter, entitled Eleusis in the early
centuries of the historic era, in which the author describes the
Geometric and Archaic remains of the sanctuary. Students,
however, will probably find the final chapter on the Eleusinian
mysteries to be the most valuable. B/C.

NEUMAYER, H. Greek vase-painting. (Movements in World Art.) New York:
Crown Publishers 1967. Pp.56; 20 pls. $.95 cloth.

A short pictorial introduction to Greek vase painting. This book
contains a short introductory essay, followed by twenty color
illustrations which show the development of vase painting from
the Geometric period to the end of the Fourth Century B.C.
Facing each plate is a brief paragraph of description and
interpretation. B.

PAUSANIAS. Guide to Greece, trans. Peter Levi. 2 vols. Baltimore:
Penguin 1971. Pp.587; 25 ill.; 8 maps (vol.1). Pp.532; 15 ill.

(vol.2). $3.25 paper (each).

A much needed and valuable translation of Pausanias' (2nd Cent.
A.D.) comprehensive guide book to Greece. The translator provides
an introduction, together with maps, plans, and copious footnotes
throughout the text. B.

POLLITT, J.J. The ancient view of Greek art. (Yale Publications in the
History of Art 26.) New Haven: Yale University Press 1974. Pp.
282. $6.95 paper.

A survey of art criticism in antiquity. In his prologue, the
author states the rationale behind his work, that knowing how
the ancient Greeks judged their own art can give us a useful
prespective in making our evaluation of it. He divides his book
into three parts, covering the areas of art criticism in antiquity
(PartI), art history in antiquity (Part II), and a lengthy
glossary of the principal Greek and Latin terms of Greek art
criticism. The paperback edition cited above contains the complete
text of the lengthier and more expensive hadrback version, but
the glossary is condensed to include only the most significant
and widely used terms. The author hopes that in this manner the book
will be helpful to the nonspecialist. Yet, since nothing has been
changed from the hardback version, the so-called student edition
in reality is understandable only to the specialist. It
presupposes a considerable amount of background knowledge and
training on the part of the reader. The nonspecialist, or the
student with little or no knowledge of the Classical languages,
will find this book extremely difficult to read. C.

POLLITT, J.J. <u>Art</u> and <u>experience</u> <u>in</u> classical <u>Greece</u>. New York:
Cambridge University Press 1972. Pp.205; 87 ill. $3.95 paper.
There has long been a need for a suitable textbook treating solely
the art and architecture of the classical period. Pollitt's book
fulfills this function. Used together with Holloway's <u>A</u> <u>View</u>
<u>of</u> <u>Greek</u> <u>Art</u> (see above), it can provide excellent required
reading for any undergraduate course on Archaic and Classical Greek
art. By "classical" the author means the period between 480 and
323 B.C. He thus includes much of the Fourth Century within the
scope of his book. The author treats the art of this period
together with its literary and historical background. Specifically,
he seeks to understand not <u>how</u> Greek art and literature are
related, but <u>why</u> they are related. Interesting side-lines, such
as the later history of the Parthenon in Byzantine and Turkish
times, are included in footnotes. Two major criticisms, however,
must be made. In the first place, the author completely neglects
the Athenian Agora together with its buildings and sculptures
(especially those of the Hephaesteum). The Agora is a vital
area for any book on classical art. Secondly, the temple of
Apollo at Bassae is not treated with sufficient depth. For
example, the author does not touch upon the problem of whether or
not the Niobid figures in Rome and Copenhagen belong to one of
the temple's pediments, and he understates the importance of
the interior frieze as a foreshadowing of Fourth Century style.
In all, however, this is an excellent book with good photographic
illustrations. A.

POLLITT, J.J. The art of Greece 1400-31 B.C.: sources and documents.
Englewood Cliffs, N.J.: Prentice-Hall 1965. Pp.254. $3.95 paper.
A collection of the most important Greek and Latin texts relating
to sculpture, painting, architecture, and the minor arts in
Greece. The author has translated the texts and provides an
introduction, commentary, and explanatory footnotes. The
chronological framework of the book is arranged according to
subject-matter and not by the date of the authors whose writings
are used. An especial attempt has been made to relate the texts
to the extant remains of Greek art and architecture. This is the
olny such work in English; the translations are of a uniformly
high quality throughout the book. B.

RICHTER, G.M.A. A handbook of Greek árt, 6th ed. New York: Phaidon
Publishers 1969. Pp.431; 520 ill. $5.95 paper.

First published in 1959.

An excellent survey of the visual arts of Greece. The author
discusses her material by topics, such as architecture, sculpture,
and vase painting, and under each topic she examines the various
chronological periods. A very welcome and unusual feature is the
inclusion of such topics as decorative metalwork, engraved gems,
coins, jewellery, furniture, textiles, glass and glaze, and
epigraphy. The emphasis of this book, however, is on sculpture.
The section on architecture is quite sketchy and could be expended
to include a fuller treatment of private houses, fortifications,
city planning, and the various types of public buildings. The
author does not even include plans of the Athenian Acropolis and
Agora, nor does she discuss the development of these areas. A/B.

ROBINSON, H.S. Corinth: a brief history of the city and a guide to
the excavations. Princeton: American School of Classical Studies
1964. Pp.15; 12 ill.; 2 plans. $.50 paper.

A concise guide book to the ancient city of Corinth, particularly
useful for the visitor to the site. The book begins with a
brief survey of the architectural development of Corinth, then
takes the visitor on a tour of the central area, and ends with
a discussion of the outlying areas of the city. B.

ROBINSON. H.S. The urban development of ancient Corinth: Princeton:
American School of Classical Studies 1965. Pp.32; 19 ill.
$.50 paper.

A survey of the urban and architectural development of Corinth
from prehistoric down to medieval times. The visitor to Corinth
will find this small book useful and informative. B.

SCHEFOLD, K. The art of classical Greece. (Art of the World.)
New York: Crown Publishers 1967. Pp.294; 49 pls.; 77 ill.
$6.95 cloth.

A survey of developments in architecture, painting, and sculpture
from 500 to 323 B.C. The author has also included the Fourth
Century B.C. within the scope of his book. The text is extremely
thorough and detailed. But, because of the proliferation of names,
dates, and monuments, students may find this book hard to read.
It is thus not recommended for class use. C.

SCRANTON, R.L. Greek architecture. New York: George Braziller 1967.
Pp.128; 111 ill. $2.95 paper.

A short introduction to the forms and esthetics of Greek
architecture from 4000 to 31 B.C. The plates at the back of
the book are excellent, but the text (only forty pages in
length) is very sketchy and will be of little help to the
student. Recommended only for brief supplementary reading. B.

SCULLY, V. The earth, the temple, and the gods, rev. ed. New York:
Praeger 1969. Pp.271; 456 ill. $5.95 paper.

First published in 1962.

A detailed critical history of Greek sacred architecture. This
is not a handbook involving the discussion of the development
of architectural forms or of the technological problems
involved, but it views Greek temples as physical embodiments
of the gods, set in landscapes that had sacred connotations.
The author thus views the Greek temple in relation to the
landscape in which it was set. There are copious illustrations,
including plans and reconstructed drawings, along with important
photographs of little knows sites. B.

SELTMAN, C. Approach to Greek art. New York: E.P. Dutton and Co.
1960. Pp.143; 111 pls.; 10 ill. $1.75 paper.

An unusual analysis of Greek art from 1650 B.C. to 800 A.D.,
arguing that the more famous artists were primarily workers in
metal, as sculptors in bronze and in gold and ivory, or as
chasers and engravers. The author also tries to relate the art
to the literature of the times. The text is dogmatic in places,
but on the whole easy to read. Many of the illustrations at the
back of the book appear for the first time in a popular work
on art. B.

THOMPSON, H.A. The Athenian agora: a guide to the excavations and
museum, 2nd ed. rev. Princeton: American School of Classical
Studies 1962. Pp.230; 18 pls.; 29 figs. No price listed. Paper.
An excellent and useful guide book to help the visitor find his
way around both the Agora excavations and the museum located in
the Stoa of Attalus. B.

WEBSTER, T.B.L. The art of Greece: the age of Hellenism. (Art of
the World.) New York: Crown Publishers 1966. Pp.243; 54 pls.;
55 ill. $6.95 cloth.

An excellent survey of Hellenistic art and architecture,
including such minor arts as terracottas, masks, coinage, and
book illustration. The author begins with a short introduction
to the political and intellectual background of the Hellenistic
age. This is the only book in such a reasonable price range to
examine solely the art of the Hellenistic period and is highly
recommended for class use. A.

WOODHEAD, A.G. The Greeks in the west. (see section VII.)

WYCHERLEY, R.E. How the Greeks built cities, 2nd ed. New York:
Doubleday and Co. 1969. Pp.251; 16 pls.; 52 ill. $1.95 paper.

First published in 1948.

A brief survey of Greek architecture concentrating upon the
structure of the Greek city and its main components. The author
defines the form which the city took and the buildings which
went into its makeup. The text is very readable with copious
plans and reconstructions. This book is highly recommended
for class use. A.

YAMAUCHI, E. <u>Greece</u> <u>and</u> <u>Babylon</u>. Grand Rapids, Michigan: Baker
Book House 1967. Pp.115; 62 ill. $1.50 paper.
An examination of the contacts between the Greeks and the peoples
of the Near East from 3000 to 400 B.C. The author bases his
work on archaeological, epigraphical, and historical evidence.
At the end of the book he includes a brief chapter on the
intellectual influences. B.

V. ETRUSCAN.

    The offerings in this field are poor indeed. There are only ten
books listed in this bibliography, and there is no paperback which
is really suitable for class use. Pallottino's The Etruscans
(Baltimore: Penguin 1955) has long been out of print. A revised
and enlarged edition of this book is due to be issued in June,
1975, by Indiana University Press. But, it will be in hardback
form and will cost $10.95. However, it is probably the most
comprehensive survey of Etruscan life and is highly recommended
for class use.

BLOCH, R. The ancient civilization of the Etruscans. New York:
    Cowles Book Co. 1969. Pp.205; 132 pls. $10.00 cloth.
    A reissue of the Etruscan volume in the Archaeologia Mundi
    series, which has been out of print. This book is primarily
    an archaeological approach to Etruscan civilization. The author
    begins by discussing the development of archaeological research
    in Etruria; he first considers the problems of Etruscan origins
    and language and then how evidence (up to 1964) is applied
    to these; finally, he examines current methods of the excavation
    of Etruscan sites. This is an unusual and welcome approach
    to Etruscology. The reader will find here little emphasis
    on art and society. The book perhaps suffers from a lack of
    plans, but the photographs are excellent. B.

BLOCH, R. The Etruscans. (see section VII.)

BRIGUET, M.-F. Etruscan art: Tarquinia frescoes. (Little Art Library
    44.) New York: Tudor Publishing Co. 1961. Pp.12; 15 pls.; 2 ill.
    $.49 paper.

A very brief survey of Etruscan painting, intended for the
general reader. An introduction of ten pages is followed by
fifteen color plates. B.

CARRA, M. Italian sculpture from prehistory to the Etruscans.
(Cameo Series.) New York: Tudor Publishing Co. 1970. Pp.159;
70 pls. $2.95 cloth.

Primarily a pictorial history of early Italian sculpture,
including selected examples from the Etruscan period. The value
of this book lies in the illustrations of the Nuraghic art of
Sardinia, many of which are reproduced here for the first time in
color. The accompanying text, however, which is interspersed
between the plates is generally sketchy and uninformative,
and no attempt has been made at cross-referencing the plates
with the text. B/C.

HENCKEN, H. Tarquinia and Etruscan origins. (see section VII.)

MANSUELLI, G.A. The art of Etruria and early Rome. (Art of the
World.) New York: Crown Publishers 1965. Pp.255; 80 pls.;
72 ill. $6.95 cloth.

This is perhaps the best general survey of Etruscan art and
architecture in such a reasonable price range. The author
begins with an introduction about the makeup of the Etruscans,
their political structure and economic life. The rest of the
book is divided up chronologically into the different periods
of Etruscan art from the early Villanovan geometric style to the
art in the Roman republic. The one major drawback to the book
is the sketchy treatment of Etruscan architecture and town
planning. For instance, there is no discussion of the town

planning at Marzabotto nor of the important ruins at Veii.
Especially lacking is a treatment of the archaeology of
early Rome and of the city's quick advance from a primitive
village settlement to an urbanized center. At times the text
is hard to read and confusing, but this is probably the result
of the translation into English from the original Italian. A/B.

RICHARDSON, E. The Etruscans. Chicago: University of Chicago Press
1964. Pp.285; 48 pls.; 4 figs. $7.95 cloth.

An examination of the art and civilization of the Etruscans.
The author begins her book with a brief discussion of Etruscan
origins and Etruscan history through the First Century B.C.
She follows this with a detailed study of the art and architecture,
ending with chpaters on language, literature, and religion.
One criticism is that more plans and photographs are needed to
accompany the text, especially the pages on architecture.
For instance, the author devotes several pages to a discussion
of the important Regolini-Galassi tomb at Caere but nowhere
provides a plan of the tomb or photographs of the finds from
the tomb. Similarly, she discusses major works of sculpture
and painting without providing photographs of them. If it were
not for these omissions, this book could be used as a class
text. Some of the photographs that she does supply, however,
are welcome in that they are not the usual ones provided in the
handbooks of Etruscan art and architecture. B.

RICHARDSON, E. Etruscan sculpture. New York; The New American
Library 1966. Pp.92; 32 pls.; 3 ill. $.95 paper.

A brief pictorial survey of Etruscan sculpture, consisting of
thirty-two color plates which are preceded by a short, but excellent,
introduction of twenty-four pages. This book will be of interest
to the general reader. B.

STRONG, D. The early Etruscans. (Life in Ancient Lands.)
New York: G.P. Putnam's Sons 1968. Pp.144; 102 ill.
$5.95 cloth.

An excellent general introduction to the art and society of
the early Etruscans from 750 to 400 B.C., a period which saw
the rise of Etruscan civilization, the maximum extension of
its power, and the beginning of its decline. This book is
thus unusual because it concentrates upon a limited period
of Etruscan history. The author discusses the art of the
Etruscans, their customs, history, and language. B.

von VACANO, O.-W. The Etruscans in the ancient world. Bloomington:
Indiana University Press 1965. Pp.195; 16 pls.; 38 ill.
$1.95 paper.

First published in 1960.

An examination of Etruscan culture divided roughly into chronological
periods. The author begins with a discussion of how closely
the life of the Etruscans was governed by their religion.
He goes on to discuss their origins, their links with the
rest of the ancient world, their conflicts with the Greeks and
Romans, and their final assimilation into the Roman state.
Unfortunately, the student and the general reader may find
that this book lacks a coherent organization and thus may

be hard to read. Furthermore, the plates in the book have been badly reproduced, and the details are quite blurred. C.

VI. ROMAN.

The largest gaps occur in this area. Compared with the offerings in Greek art, those in Roman art are quite meager. For instance, there is no paperback handbook of Roman art and no paperback work on Roman sculpture. And those on architecture and painting are really inadequate for class use.

BARFIELD, L.H. Northern Italy before Rome. (see section VII.)

BLOCH, R. The origins of Rome.

BROWN, F.E. Roman architecture. New York: George Braziller 1961. Pp. 127; 100 ill. $2.95 paper.

A very brief survey (40 pages of text) of the problem of space in Roman architecture. This book is not a review of the methods, techniques, and surviving monuments of Roman architecture, but rather a discussion of how the Romans used space and shaped it around their ritualistic and habitual forms of behavior. The plates at the back of the book are excellent. B.

COLLEDGE, M.A.R. The Parthians. (see section VII.)

COLLINGWOOD, R.G. Roman Britain, corr. ed. New York: Oxford University Press 1953. Pp. 160; 59 ill. $4.25 cloth.

First published in 1923.

A brief general introduction to the archaeology and history of Roman Britain, written with a view to the student and the general reader. The author discusses such topics as the history of the occupation, town and country life, art and language, and religion. B.

COTTRELL, L. A guide to Roman Britain. Philadelphia: Chilton Company
1966. Pp. 337; 44 ill. $6.95 cloth.

First published in 1956.

A popular guide book to Roman Britain. The author writes in
personal terms describing his own travels throughout Roman Britain.
Each chapter deals with a particular tour and includes a description of the route taken and the sites visited. At the end of the
book there is a supplementary chapter on recent discoveries from
1955 to 1965. This book, however, is not in the same class with
Bean's archaeological guides to Greco-Roman sites in Turkey
(see section IV). For instance, there are few maps to indicate
to the traveller where he is going, and there are no plans to
guide him around the important sites. Also, the photographs at
the back are almost useless, because they are extremely dark and
underdeveloped. B.

DEISS, J.J. Herculaneum: Italy's buried treasure. New York: Thomas
Y. Crowell Co. 1970. Pp. 174; 74 ill. $4.95 paper.

First published in 1966.

A popular survey of the history of Herculaneum, its monuments, and
the life of its people. The author is a novelist who writes with
a view to using the finds for reconstructing the life of the city.
The last chapter presents a graphic picture of the immense
difficulties facing Italian archaeology. There are numerous black
and white photographs. B.

GUIDO, M. Sardinia. (see section VII.)

HAFNER, G. <u>The art of Rome</u>, <u>Etruria</u>, <u>and Magna Graecia</u>. New York:
Harry Abrams 1969. Pp. 264; 251 ill. $7.95 cloth.
A pictorial history of art and architecture in Italy and Sicily
from the Eighth Century B.C. to the early Fourth Century A.D.
There is a brief introduction of seven pages. The rest of the
book consists of illustrations arranged in chronological order.
Next to each illustration the author places a brief description
and makes comments about identification and style. The same criticism
which applies to the author's <u>Art of Crete</u>, <u>Mycenae</u>, <u>and Greece</u>
(see section IV) is also valid here, namely the lack of attention
paid to architecture and architectural forms. The 108 color plates,
however, are especially good. B.

KÄHLER, H. <u>The art of Rome and her empire</u>. (Art of the World.) New
York: Crown Publishers 1965. Pp. 259; 79 pls.; 46 ill. $6.95 cloth.
An excellent survey of Roman Imperial art and architecture from
Augustus to Constantine. Of special interest is the first chapter
on the fundamental characteristics of Roman art. Throughout the
entire book, the author stresses the unique quality of Roman art
and culture, despite the many outside influences. One omission,
however, is the complete neglect of any discussion of the important
area of mosaics -- an area which is vital to any survey of Roman
art, since the Romans were in effect responsible for the development
of this medium. There are copious plans and drawings and good photographic material. This book is highly recommended for class use. A.

LITTLE, A.M.G. Roman perspective painting and the ancient stage. Kennebunk, Maine: Star Press, Inc. 1971. Pp. 50; 11 pls. $3.00 paper.

This is the third of the author's works on the archaeology of the
ancient theater and its social implications. The first two are
called Plautus and Popular Drama and Myth and Society in Athenian
Drama. This third volume seeks to examine the parallels existing
between certain Fourth Style walls at Pompeii and the stone facades
of the Roman stage. The author divides his book into three parts:
in the first, he discusses early scenography and what the term stood
for in antiquity; in the second, he treats architecture and perspective in Roman painting. This topic, of course, has been examined
before, but the author presents here a good review of the evidence.
Especially interesting, however, is the third part, entitled A Painted
Sourcebook for the Roman Stage, in which he looks at the various
paintings which illustrate the Roman stage, including a discussion
of the recently discovered (1960) paintings at the Room of the Masks
in the House of Augustus on the Palatine. This book is a good review
of the evidence for the ancient stage in Roman painting. Unfortunatel
several of the plates at the back have been badly reproduced. B.

LITTLE, A.M.G. A Roman bridal drama at the Villa of the Mysteries.
Kennebunk, Maine: Star Press, Inc. 1972. Pp. 47; 11 pls. $3.00
paper.

A companion piece to Roman Perspective Painting and the Ancient Stage,
this book examines not only the cycle of paintings in the Villa of
the Mysteries at Pompeii but also the definition and use of the term

<u>megalographia</u> (large figure painting) in Roman painting in general.
This is a useful book but is hampered by the dark and muggy plates
at the back. C.

LIVERSIDGE, J. <u>Furniture</u> <u>in</u> <u>Roman</u> <u>Britain</u>. Levittown, N.Y.: Transatlantic Arts, Inc. 1955. Pp. 76; 69 pls.; 5 ill. $3.00 cloth.
An interesting monograph on Roman furniture and furniture types in
Britain. This book is easy to read and can serve as a good introduction to Roman furniture in general. B.

L'ORANGE, H.P. <u>Art</u> <u>forms</u> <u>and</u> <u>civic</u> <u>life</u> <u>in</u> <u>the</u> <u>late</u> <u>Roman</u> <u>empire</u>.
Princeton: Princeton University Press 1965. Pp. 131; 67 ill.
$5.00 cloth

   First published in 1958.
An examination of the parallel development between the style and form
of art and the changes made by Diocletian in the political structure
of the empire. The author discusses the emergence of a strict
geometric planning in architecture, an impressionism in portrait
sculpture, and a certain exaggerated rigidity in relief sculpture. B.

McDONALD, A.H. <u>Republican</u> <u>Rome</u>. (see section VII.)

McKAY, A.G. <u>Naples</u> <u>and</u> <u>Campania</u>. Hamilton, Ontario: The Vergilian
Society of America 1962. Pp. 265; 16 pls.; 17 ill. $3.50 paper.
A useful guide book to the major historical sites and monuments of
Campania and Lucania. The author introduces each site with a brief
historical sketch and then examines the archaeological remains,
ending with a discussion of the literary references. Indeed, the
emphasis of this book is on the literary sources and what they tell

us about the ancient sites. B.

MacKENDRICK, P. The Dacian stones speak. Chapel Hill, N.C.: University
of North Carolina Press 1975. Pp. 272; 161 ill. $12.95 cloth.
This is the most recent in the author's series of cultural histories
based on archaeological evidence (the others are The Mute, Greek,
and Iberian Stones Speak, Romans on the Rhine, and Roman France).
This book examines the history and archaeology of Romania (the
ancient province of Dacia) from Neolithic times to the end of
Roman rule. B.

MacKENDRICK, P. The Iberian stones speak. New York: Funk and Wagnalls
1969. Pp. 238; 155 ill. $7.95 cloth.
A well written and unusual account of the story of archaeology in
Spain and Portugal. The author attempts to reconstruct the cultural
history of the Iberian peninsula from the archaeological remains.
He pays especial attention to the pre-Roman remains and emphasizes
the persistence of the Iberian tradition under Roman rule. This is
the only such book in English and will be useful both to students and
to the archaeologically minded traveller. B.

MacKENDRICK, P. The mute stones speak. New York: The New American
Library 1966. Pp. 360; 171 ill. $.95 paper.
First published in 1960.
An excellent account of the story of archaeology in Italy from prehistoric times to the reign of Constantine. The author's purpose is
to reconstruct the cultural history of Italy from the archaeological
remains. He concentrates heavily on the architecture and the building

but pays relatively little attention to sculpture and painting.
Highly recommended for students. A.

MacKENDRICK, P. Roman France. New York: St. Martin's Press 1972.
Pp. 275; 128 ill. $10.95 cloth.

An account of the Roman presence and influence on France. Since it
is really the only such book of its kind which presents a general
survey of the Roman ruins in France, it can also be used as a guidebook to the archaeological sites in France. The author here uses his
customary procedure of combining the literary, historical, and archaeological evidence to present an over-all picture of Roman France.
Especially interesting is the last chapter which discusses Roman-
inspired architecture in modern France. Perhaps the weakest of the
chapters is the first on France before the Romans. Unfortunately, the
author uses this chapter simply to present background information and
does not delve too deeply into the very interesting Greek ruins in
France. Especially important are the recent excavations behind the
Stock Exchange at Marseille which have uncovered portions of the city
walls and the Hellenistic public and private buildings at Glanum. B.

MacKENDRICK, P. Romans on the Rhine. New York: Funk and Wagnalls 1970.
Pp. 269; 170 ill. $7.95 cloth.

A very good account of the story of Roman archaeology in Germany. The
author broadens the scope set by his title by including selected sites
from parts of Holland, Switzerland, Austria, Hungary, and West Germany.
His purpose is the same as that in The mute stones speak, namely to
write a cultural history based upon the archaeological remains.

This is the only such book in English and will be useful to students and travellers alike. B.

MAIURI, A. Pompeian wall paintings. (Orbis Pictus 4.) New York: Taplinger Publishing Co. n.d. Pp. 47; 19 pls. $2.50 cloth.

A small selection of Roman paintings intended for the general reader. This book consists of 19 color photographs of various wall paintings from Pompeii and Herculaneum. Facing each photograph is a page containing remarks about identification and style. The entire collection of plates is prefaced by a short general introduction of seven pages.

MICHALOWSKI, K. Palmyra. New York: Praeger 1970. Pp. 30; 88 pls. $7.50 cloth.

A good general survey of the history and main monuments of Palmyra. The author pays especial attention to the results of recent Polish excavations in the city. The copious photographs at the back of the book are superb. This book can be used both by the visitor to the area and by students for supplementary reading. B.

MORGAN, M.H. Vitruvius: the ten books on architecture. New York: Dover Publications 1960. Pp. 331; 68 ill. $2.00 paper.

First published in 1914.

A good translation of Vitruvius' work on Greek and Roman architecture. The value of this book lies in the many plates and drawings which have been inserted into the work to illustrate the text. B.

PAGET, R.F. Central Italy: an archaeological guide. Park Ridge, N.J.: The Noyes Press 1973. Pp.256; 35 pls.; 17 figs.; 19 plans and maps.

A guide to the Etruscan and Roman remains of Central Italy, an area

bounded on the north by Florence and on the south by Naples. This
book will be of interest to the traveller to these regions since it
is organized with plenty of relevant tourist information, including
an alphabetized list of museums and a short, but useful, glossary of
terms at the back. One drawback, however, is that many of the plates
appear to be quite dark and consequently it is difficult to make out
details in them. B.

PICARD, G. The ancient civilization of Rome. New York: Cowles Book Co.
1969. Pp. 283; 192 pls. $10.00 cloth.

A reissue of the Roman volume in the Archaeologia Mundi series, which
has been out of print. This book is primarily an archaeological approach
to Roman civilization. In the first part, the author discusses the
history of Roman archaeology up to about 1960, starting from the beginnings at Pompeii and Herculaneum, and then ranging further afield
to Africa, Syria, Asia Minor, Spain, and Central Europe. The second
part consists of an examination of the problems and methods of Roman
archaeology. The book suffers from a lack of plans, but contains
good photographs, especially of some unfamiliar material (partly from
Carthage) in the Bardo Museum at Tunis. Because of its emphasis on
finds of sculpture and painting, it is perhaps best read in conjunction with MacKendrick's The mute stones speak, which concentrates on
the architecture and the buildings of the Roman era. B.

PICARD, G. Living architecture: Roman. New York: Grosset and Dunlap
1965. Pp. 192; 84 pls.; 36 plans. $7.95 cloth.

An attempt to dispel the idea of uniformity in Roman buildings and to show that the architecture was not fixed and rigid but continually producing new solutions. Unfortunately, the layout of this book is confusing. The discussion jumps quickly from one subject to another, and the usefulness of the very good plans and photographs is minimized by their haphazard arrangement throughout the text and by the fact that they are not cross-referenced with the appropriate passages in the text. C.

POLLITT, J.J. The art of Rome 753 B.C. - 337 A.D.: sources and documents Englewood Cliffs, N.J.: Prentice-Hall 1966. Pp. 251; 3 ill. $3.95 paper.

A collection of the most important ancient texts relating to Roman art and architecture. This is the first such collection of literary testimonia for the sculpture and painting of the Empire. The author has translated the texts and provides explanatory footnotes. For each period he includes a fairly extensive historical introduction which provides background material for the non-specialist. B.

RICHMOND, I.A. Roman Britain, 2nd ed. (The Pelican History of England 1.) Baltimore: Penguin 1963. Pp. 240; 8 pls.; 12 ill. $1.25 paper.

First published in 1955.

A general survey of the archaeology and history of Roman Britain from the conquest of Claudius in 43 A.D. to the Fifth Century A.D. The author does not attempt to provide a continuous historical account but concentrates upon the military organization of the island. He also discusses such topics as the urban centers, the countryside, the economics of the province, and the religious cults. B.

RICHTER, G.M.A. Roman portraits. New York: Metropolitan Museum of Art

1948. Pp. 69; 110 ill. $2.00 paper.

A survey of the Roman portraits in the Metropolitan Museum of Art

in New York. The portraits are arranged in chronological order;

the whole collection is prefaced by a brief introduction of five

pages. This is a useful book, since the entire development of Roman

portraiture can be seen from these examples in the Metropolitan

Museum. B.

SORRELL, A. Roman London. New York: Arco Publishing Co. 1969. Pp. 71;

60 ill. $6.50 cloth.

A very clear account, designed for the general reader, of life in

Roman London. The especial value of this book lies in the 18 recon-

structed drawings of the city made by the author. These drawings,

coupled with plans and photographs of objects found in London, give

a good picture of what the city was like in Roman times. B.

STENICO, A. Roman and Etruscan painting. (Compass History of Art 2.)

New York: Viking Press 1963. Pp. 218; 176 ill. $2.25 paper.

A pictorial survey of Etruscan and Roman painting. The majority of

this book consists of plates, many of them in color, illustrating the

historical development of Roman and Etruscan painting. At the beginning

there is an excellent introduction of forty-one pages. The examples

(including quite a number of mosaics) which the author discusses are

helpfully cross-listed with the appropriate plates at the back. This

book is highly recommended·for supplementary reading. B.

STRONG, D.E. <u>Roman imperial sculpture</u>. Levittown, N.Y.: Transatlantic
Arts, Inc. 1961. Pp. 104; 144 pls. $9.00 cloth.

A good introduction to the commemorative and decorative sculpture of
the Roman empire down to the death of Constantine. The plates at the
back are especially good. This is the only book of its kind in such
a reasonable price range and is highly recommended for supplementary
reading. B.

TOYNBEE, J.M.C. <u>The art of the Romans</u>. (see section VII.)

TRUMP, D.H. <u>Central and southern Italy</u>. (see section VII.)

WHEELER, M. <u>Roman art and architecture</u>. New York: Praeger 1964.
Pp. 250; 215 ill. $3.95 paper.

A very witty and readable general introduction to Roman art and archi
tecture. The author, concentrating upon the uniqueness of the Roman
achievement, does not confine himself to Italy by ranges far afield
throughout the empire. He pays especial attention to architecture an
city planning, and as a result sculpture, painting, and mosaics are
treated rather sketchily but still in enough depth to allow the book
to serve as a suitable text for class use. A.

WISEMAN, J. <u>Stobi: a guide to the excavations</u>. Published by the
University of Texas at Austin and the National Museum of Titov
Veles, Belgrade, Yugoslavia 1973. Pp. 83; 21 figs.; 1 plan. $3.50
paper.

A good guide to the history and monuments at Stobi, designed primaril
to guide the traveler around the ruins. Especially valuable is the

bibliography with which the author ends the description of each major monument or building. B.

VII. MISCELLANEOUS.

This section consists of a heterogeneous group of books which deserve mention but not lengthy critical comments. The entries from the Ancient Peoples and Places series should especially be noted. They are all of a uniformly high quality and are recommende for supplementary reading. Other categories include novels and periodicals.

BARFIELD, L.H. Northern Italy before Rome. (Ancient Peoples and Places 76.) New York: Praeger 1972. Pp. 208; 73 pls.; 69 figs.; 12 maps. $12.50 cloth.

BASS, G.F. Archaeology under water. (Ancient Peoples and Places 48.) New York: Praeger 1966. Pp. 224; 62 pls.; 47 figs. $8.50 cloth. An excellent introduction to the methods and techniques of underwater archaeology. The author examines such topics as working in the under water environment, underwater search and survey, raising operations, and the salvaging of artifacts. He also discusses some of the import statuary that has been found under water. In 1970, Penguin Books issued a paperback version of this book (see section II). B.

BROTHWELL, D. and P. Food in antiquity. (Ancient Peoples and Places 66.) New York: Praeger 1969. Pp. 200; 67 pls.; 45 figs. $8.50 cloth. A comparative survey of the human diet in ancient societies. The authors discuss all types of foods, including the vertebrates and invertebrates, sugar, cereals, vegetables, fruits, and drinks. The 1 chapter contains an interesting discussion of diet and disease. B.

BERN' ꟁ BREA, L. <u>Sicily</u> <u>before</u> <u>the</u> <u>Greeks</u>. (Ancient Peoples and Places 3.)
New York: Praeger 1966. Pp. 255; 78 pls.; 50 figs.; 7 maps. $8.50
cloth.

An excellent and comprehensive account of Sicilian prehistory from the
Palaeolithic period to the time of the founding of the Greek colonies.
This is the only such book in English, but it lacks detailed architec-
tural plans and needs to undergo revision to include recent discoveries.
(a revised edition has appeared in Italian, but not as yet in English.)
C.

BLEGEN, C.W. <u>Troy</u> <u>and</u> <u>the</u> <u>Trojans</u>. (Ancient Peoples and Places 33.)
New York: Praeger 1963. Pp. 240; 67 pls.; 42 figs. $8.50 cloth.
A concise account of the civilization of Bronze Age Troy. The author
discusses the major periods of the occupation of Troy and presents the
results of his excavations at Troy from 1932 to 1938, reporting the
significant finds and the evidence for the different periods of Trojan
history. This book contains good detailed plans and is highly recommended. B.

BLOCH, R. <u>The</u> <u>Etruscans</u>, rev ed. (Ancient Peoples and Places 7.) New York:
Praeger 1961. Pp. 260; 79 pls.; 41 figs. $8.50 cloth.
An archaeological and cultural survey of the Etruscans. The author
examines the literary and archaeological evidence, and discusses their
art and architecture, their institutions and customs, and their religion.
He also deals with two great problems: that of the Etruscan origins
and that of their relationship to Greece and Rome. This book should
be of interest to both the general reader and to students. However,

it needs to undergo a second revision to take into account recent

discoveries and to include architectural plans and drawings. B.

BLOCH, R. The origins of Rome. (Ancient Peoples and Places 15.) New York

Praeger 1960. Pp. 212; 60 pls.; 22 figs. $8.50 cloth.

An excellent general introduction to the archaeology and history of

early Rome. The author discusses the different peoples and civiliza-

tions of prehistoric Italy, the first human settlements on the site of

Rome, the Etruscan settlement there, and the languages, law, and

religion of the primitive city. Unfortunately, the book needs a

revision to include recent discoveries. B.

COLLEDGE, M.A.R. The Parthians. (Ancient Peoples and Places 59.) New Yor

Praeger 1967. Pp. 243; 76 pls.; 48 figs. $8.50 cloth.

A very important general introduction to the culture of the Parthians,

the only such book in English written with a view to the student and

the general reader. The author presents a rounded picture of the

Parthians but emphasizes their political history, much of it drawn

from archaeological sources. The excavations of the past forty years

have also added greatly to our knowledge of Parthian art and architec-

ture, which the author discusses. B.

COOK, J.M. The Greeks in Ionia and the east. (Ancient Peoples and Places

31.) New York: Praeger 1963. Pp. 268; 76 pls.; 53 figs. $8.50 clot

A general survey of the architectural, artistic, and historical achiev

ments of the Greek cities in Asia Minor and the east from the first

migrations in the 11th Century B.C. to the succession of Alexander the

Great. There is a brief epilogue on the Roman rule of the east.

This is the only such survey in English, and students may find it
useful. However, it needs to be revised to take into account recent
discoveries and to include more architectural plans. B.

COOK, R.M. The Greeks until Alexander. (Ancient Peoples and Places 24.)
New York: Praeger 1962. Pp. 264; 89 pls.; 39 figs. $8.50 cloth.
A survey of Greek civilization from the early Iron Age to the advent
of Alexander the Great. The author discusses all the various aspects
of the different periods of the civilization on the Greek mainland,
such as architecture, art, economics, literature, politics, religion,
and society. The illustrations show the appearance today of the sites
and sanctuaries discussed in the book and provide a short survey of
Greek art. A.

GUIDO, M. Sardinia. (Ancient Peoples and Places 35.) New York: Praeger
1964. Pp. 277; 77 pls.; 61 figs. $8.50 cloth.
This is the only book in English dealing with Sardinian prehistory
from the time of the earliest settlers from the Eastern Mediterranean
to the Phoenician settlements. It contains good plans and drawings. B.

HENCKEN, H. Tarquinia and Etruscan origins. (Ancient Peoples and Places
62.) New York: Praeger 1968. Pp. 248; 173 pls.; 50 figs. $8.50 cloth.
An important examination of the early days of Tarquinia. The author
looks at the Villanovan (ca. 1000-700 B.C.) material found in the tombs
at Tarquinia and examines the various elements that make up the Villanovan civilization of Tarquinia, including Balkan, Central European,
and Aegean elements. He ends his book with a chapter on the origins
of the Villanovans and Etruscans. B.

HOOD, S. The Minoans. (Ancient Peoples and Places 75.) New York: Praege

1971   Pp. 239; 120 pls.; 131 figs. $9.50 cloth.

A comprehensive survey of the Minoan civilization on Crete. This boo

is well organized and easy to read. The author begins with the trans

tion from the Neolithic to the Bronze Age and then discusses the evi-

dence for the chronology of the various periods. He includes an impo

tant chapter on happenings and events in which he turns to such

problems as the end of the early palaces (ca. 1700 B.C.), the erup-

tion of Thera (ca. 1500 B.C.), and the last palace at Knossos. Sub-

seqent chapters include such topics as buildings, food and cloths,

arts and crafts, war and trade, and burial customs. This book con-

tains good plans and photographs. B.

McDONALD, A.H. Republican Rome. (Ancient Peoples and Places 50.)

New York: Praeger 1966. Pp. 244; 87 pls.; 21 figs. $8.50 cloth.

A survey of the art, architecture, and history of Rome from the rule

of the kings to the founding of the empire by Augustus. The author

pays especial attention to the social conditions of the ruling nobles

and to the character of the Italians who were admitted to Roman

citizenship. In addition, he includes chapters on the monuments of

Republican Rome and the archaeological evidence for Roman Italy.

Unfortunately, this book lacks detailed architectural plans but con-

tains good photographs. A.

TAYLOUR, W.D. The Mycenaeans. (Ancient Peoples and Places 39.) New York

Praeger 1964. Pp. 243; 66 pls.; 74 figs. $8.50 cloth.

A general introduction to Mycenaean civilization. The author does
not use the chronological approach, but divides his subjects into a
number of cultural topics, such as the written sources, religion and
burial customs, daily life and the arts, and war and trade. The last
chapter pulls everything together in a brief historical resume of the
period. This book contains good plans and drawings but needs to undergo a revision to include recent discoveries. B.

TOYNBEE, J.M.C. The art of the Romans. (Ancient Peoples and Places 43.)
New York: Praeger 1965. Pp. 271; 91 pls. $8.50 cloth.
An excellent introduction to Roman art intended for the student and
general reader who have some knowledge of Roman history and literature.
The author discusses sculpture, painting, and mosaics, with a brief
epilogue on the minor arts, but she excludes architecture from the
scope of her book. This book is very good on the art of the Empire,
but a little weak on that of Republican Rome. A.

TRUMP, D.H. Central and southern Italy. (Ancient Peoples and Places 47.)
New York: Praeger 1966. Pp. 244; 81 pls.; 60 figs. $8.50 cloth.
An important study of the prehistory of central and southern Italy
(from the Palaeolithic to the early Iron Ages). This is the only
such survey in English; the text is well organized, and the information is clearly presented. B.

WOODHEAD, A.G. The Greeks in the west. (Ancient Peoples and Places 28.)
New York: Praeger 1962. Pp. 243; 81 pls.; 26 figs. $8.50 cloth.
An excellent archaeological and historical survey of the Greek cities

in Sicily and Southern Italy. The author attempts to isolate and to
explain the distinctive features of <u>Magna</u> <u>Graecia</u> and to asses its
relationship with mainland Greece. This is the only such general
survey in English (currently in print), but it should be revised to
include recent archaeological discoveries. B.

There are so many novels about the ancient world, that to attempt to
include them all would exceed the limits of this bibliography. Those by
Mary Renault, however, are especially good and are constructed with the
aid of archaeological evidence.

RENAULT, M. <u>The</u> <u>bull</u> <u>from</u> <u>the</u> <u>sea</u>. New York: Modern Library 1968.
Pp. 343. $2.95 cloth.

First published in 1962.

RENAULT, M. <u>Fire</u> <u>from</u> <u>heaven</u>. New York: Popular Library 1970. Pp. 381.
$1.25 paper.

First published in 1969.

RENAULT, M. <u>The</u> <u>king</u> <u>must</u> <u>die</u>. New York: Pocket Books, Inc. 1965.
Pp. 375. $.90 paper.

First published in 1958.

RENAULT, M. <u>The</u> <u>last</u> <u>of</u> <u>the</u> <u>wine</u>. New York: Pocket Books, Inc. 1964.
Pp. 372. $.95 paper.

First published in 1956.

RENAULT, M. <u>The</u> <u>mask</u> <u>of</u> <u>Apollo</u>. New York: Pocket Books, Inc. 1967.
Pp. 327. $.95 paper.

RENAULT, M. The Persian boy. New York: Bantam Books, Inc. 1974. Pp.
469. $1.95 paper.

YOURCENAR, M. Memoirs of Hadrian. New York: Farrar, Straus and Giroux,
Inc. 1963. Pp. 347; 45 ill. $4.50 paper.

(It is recommended that for a more complete listing of historical novels
about the ancient world the reader consult the annual listings in the
American Classical Review.)

Two magazines of exceptional quality should be mentioned. Archaeology,
published by the Archaeological Institute of America, 260 West Broadway,
New York, N.Y. 10013, is a periodical specifically designed for the
general reader. The articles are well illustrated and are not confined
to Greek and Roman archaeology but include all other fields, such as
American, Islamic, Near Eastern, and Oriental archaeology. There are
four issues per year. The yearly subscription rate is $8.50; the price
for single issues is $3.00. On occasion, National Geographic Magazine
contains articles of an archaeological nature, lavishly illustrated.

APPENDIX (NO. 1) ON ANCIENT URBANISM AND URBAN PLANNING

Because the area of ancient urbanism and urban planning is such an
important one and because practically no paperback books or hardbacks
under $10.00 have appeared in this field, it has been thought necessary
to compile a brief appendix of books written on the subject. Of
necessity, the principles of the bibliography have been violated, in
that books above $10.00 have been mentioned and that one written in
French has been included.

BOETHIUS, A. The golden house of Nero. Ann Arbor: University of Michigan
Press 1960. Pp. 195; 109 ill. $15.00 cloth.
An excellent survey of Roman city planning. The author begins with
Etruscan urbanization, then passes on to a discussion of the Hellenized
Italic town, Nero's golden house itself, and finally examines the
urban planning of the Imperial Age with reference to its influence
on the plans of medieval cities. B.

BOETHIUS, A. and WARD-PERKINS, J.B. Etruscan and Roman architecture.
(Pelican History of Art Series.) Baltimore: Penguin 1970. Pp. 622;
275 pls.; 204 figs. $29.50 cloth.
A comprehensive and well-written treatment of Etruscan and Roman
architecture. Part I on Etruscan architecture is especially welcome,
since this is the only such survey in English. The author treats not
only the temples and the tombs, but also he discusses town planning,
domestic architecture, and roads and bridges. Parts II and III deal

with architecture in Rome and the provinces. A brief section at the
end (Part IV) covers late pagan architecture. This book is well-
illustrated with plans, drawings, and photographs, and is highly
recommended for supplementary reading. B.

HILL, I.T. The ancient city of Athens. Chicago: Argonaut 1969. Pp. 258;
2 pls.; 34 ill. $10.00 cloth.

   First published in 1953.

A comprehensive survey of the architecture and topography of ancient
Athens from the Bronze Age to Roman times. The author concentrates
on the Acropolis and the Agora, but the last three chapters deal with
monuments further afield, such as the area west of the Acropolis, the
outskirts, and Roman Athens. This book contains good plans, but lacks
photographs and should undergo a revision to incorporate recent discoveries, especially those in the Agora. C.

LAWRENCE, A.W. Greek architecture, 2nd ed. (The Pelican History of Arts
Series.) Baltimore: Penguin 1967. Pp. 388; 152 pls.; 171 figs.;
3 maps. $20.00 cloth.

A good survey of Greek architecture from Neolithic times to the
Hellenistic period. What is unusual in this book is the considerable
space devoted to Fourth Century and Hellenistic architecture, in
which the author discusses such topics as masonry and vaulting,
residential buildings, and town planning. It contains copious plans
and reconstructed drawings, some appearing for the first time in a
general survey. The plates at the back of the book are of superior
quality. B.

MARTIN, R. L'Urbanisme dans la Grèce antique. Paris: A. and J. Picard 1956. Pp. 301; 32 pls.; 64 figs. Approx. $10.50 paper.

Perhaps the most important and comprehensive book on Greek city planning. The author discusses the principles of Greek city planning, the architectural evolution of the Greek city, and its components. This book contains good detailed plans, reconstructed drawings, and photographs of models of various cities. B.

RIDER, B.C. Ancient Greek houses. Chicago: Argonaut 1964. Pp. 272; 53 figs. $10.00 cloth.

First published in 1916.

A survey of the archaeological and literary evidence for Greek houses. Unfortunately, the text is hopelessly out of date. The author devotes most of her time to a discussion of Minoan and Mycenaean houses, but reserves very little space for those of Classical and Hellenistic times. Many of the plans also need revision. This book is best used for the author's discussion of the literary evidence for Greek houses. C.

ROBERTSON, D.S. Greek and Roman architecture. (see section I.)

WHEELER, M. Roman art and architecture. (see section VI.)

WYCHERLEY, R.E. How the Greeks built cities. (see section IV.)

APPENDIX (NO.2) ON USEFUL HARDCOVER EDITIONS ABOVE $10.00.

Since there are a number of important hardcover editions above our
price limit of $10.00, we have thought to include a selection
(published by both American and English publishers) which would be
most useful to the student and general reader. The grouping of the
books follows in general the seven divisions of the main text, but
for the sake of conciseness and greater flexibility the books have
been divided into groups and comments have been made about each
group. Again, the reader should be ware of the prices which change
so frequently that it is difficult to keep track of them. This is
especially true of books published in Great Britain. Due to the
fluctuation of the dollar, the exchange rate changes daily, and
thus it is impossible to quote a fixed price for English books.

(1) BECATTI, G. The art of ancient Greece and Rome. New York: Harry
Abrams 1967. Pp. 441; 385 ill. $30.00 cloth.

(2) FEHL, P. The classical monument: reflections on the connection between
morality and art in Greek and Roman sculpture. (College Art Association
monographs.) New York: New York University Press 1971. Pp. 115;
63 pls. $15.00 cloth.

(3) HANFMANN, G.M.A. Classical sculpture. (History of Western Sculpture,
vol.1.) Greenwich, Conn.: New York Graphic Society, Ltd. 1967.
Pp. 352; 348 monochrome pls.; 8 color pls. $14.95 cloth.

The above group of three books represents studies on both Greek and
Roman art in the same volume. As is the case with the paperbacks
on the same subject, the Roman section is overshadowed by the Greek

part. This is especially evident in Becatti's work (1) where the emphasis is on sculpture at the expense of painting and mosaics, especially of the Roman period. Indeed, a serious weakness of this book is the lack of attention paid to mosaic decoration, both Greek and Roman. There have been a number of important new finds in this field and evidence has come to light recently for the transition from the pebble to the tessera techniques. The illustrations, however, are excellent. Hanfmann (3) concentrates solely on Greek and Roman sculpture. His book is more of a pictorial history with each plate containing a paragraph of discussion. Unfortunately, these paragraphs are quite sketchy and often bypass controversial problems of identification and dating. Fehl's book (2) on the connection between morality and art in Greek and Roman sculpture is quite inconclusive. At times the author's argumentation is difficult to follow, and thus the book is not recommended for class use.

(4) ARIAS, P.E. and HIRMER, M. A history of 1,000 years of Greek vase painting. New York: Harry Abrams, Inc. 1962. Pp. 410; 240 monochrome pls.; 52 color pls. $35.00 cloth.

(5) BERVE, H. and HIRMER, M. Greek temples, theaters and shrines. New York: Harry Abrams, Inc. 1962. Pp. 508; 176 monochrome pls.; 36 color pls.; 154 figs. $30.00 cloth.

(6) BOARDMAN, J. Greek gems and finger rings: early bronze age to late classical. New York: Roy Publishers, Inc. 1970. Pp. 458; 1016 monochrome pls.; 51 color pls.; 318 figs. $29.98 cloth.

(7) BOARDMAN, J.,DÖRIG, J., FUCHS, W. and HIRMER, M. Greek art and architec

New York: Harry Abrams, Inc. 1967. Pp. 600; 320 monochrome pls.;
50 color pls.; 189 figs. $28.50 cloth.

(8) KRAAY, C.M. and HIRMER, M. Greek coins. New York: Harry Abrams,
Inc. 1966. Pp. 396; 220 monochrome pls.; 20 color pls. $30.00 cloth.

(9) LANGLOTZ, E. and HIRMER, M. Ancient Greek sculpture of southern
Italy and Sicily. New York: Harry Abrams, Inc. 1965. Pp. 312;
168 monochrome pls.; 20 color pls. $25.00 cloth.

(10) LULLIES, R. and HIRMER, M. Greek sculpture, rev. ed. New York:
Harry Abrams, Inc. 1957. Pp. 115; 282 monochrome pls.; 11 color
pls.; 12 figs. $22.50 cloth, $13.95 paper.

(11) MARINATOS, S. and HIRMER, M. Crete and Mycenae. New York: Harry
Abrams, Inc. 1960. Pp. 177; 236 monochrome pls.; 43 color pls.
$25.00 cloth.

The above constitute a large and very expensive series of picture
books dealing with certain aspects of Greek art. The best part about
these books are the superb monochrome and color plates. (Max Hirmer
is the photographer in all instances, except in no.6 where the
photographs were taken by Robert L. Wilkins.) These photographs can
be used by students to study for tests or to review course material.
The general reader will find them helpful, for they present in detail
the major aspects of Greek art. Of all the eight books, that by
Boardman, Dürig, and Fuchs (7) is perhaps the best; it is an excellent
survey of all periods of Greek art and architecture, enhanced by
good photographs. It is one of the very few works on Greek art that
treats equally all periods. The text is clearly written, and the
authors do not hesitate to discuss major problems of interpretation

and style. In all, this is one of the best handbooks on Greek art; one only wishes that it were in a more accessible price range. Boardman's other book (6) is also weee-written and can be used with equal profit by students and the general reader. Those by Arias (4), Berve (5), and Kraay (8) are all of a uniformly high quality, although a few of the color plates accompanying Berve's text are a little fuzzy. On the other hand, the books by Langlotz (9) and Lullies (10) are rather sketchy. The latter especially needs to include more Fourth Century and Hellenistic sculpture. The plates are followed by explanatory notes at the back. These confine themselves in most cases to a stylistic analysis. Problems of identification and dating are glossed over. This tends to give the student a one-sided view of Greek sculpture. Marinatos' book (11) is valuable in that it contains photographs of material not included in the usual handbooks. All eight books can be assigned for supplementary reading.

(12) BRILLIANT, R. Arts of the ancient Greeks. New York: McGraw-Hill 1972. Pp.406; 464 ill. $16.95 cloth.

(13) CHARBONNEAUX, J., MARTIN, R. and VILLARD, F. Archaic Greek art 620-480 B.C. (Arts of Mankind series.) New York: George Braziller, Inc. 1971. Pp. 438; 444 ill. $30.00 cloth.

(14) CHARBONNEAUX, J., MARTIN, R. and VILLARD, F. Classical Greek art 480-330 B.C. (Arts of Mankind series.) New York: George Braziller, Inc. 1973. Pp. 423; 345 monochrome pls.; 63 color pls.; 28 plans. $35.00 cloth.

(15) CHARBONNEAUX, J., MARTIN, R. and VILLARD, F. Hellenistic art
330-50 B.C. (Arts of Mankind series.) New York: George Braziller,
Inc. 1973. Pp. 421; 313 monochrome pls.; 76 color pls.; 32 plans.
$35.00 cloth.

(16) DEMARGNE, P. The birth of Greek art. (Arts of Mankind series.)
New York: George Braziller, Inc. 1964. Pp. 449; 538 ill.; 2 maps.
$30.00 cloth.

(17) SCHODER, R.V. Masterpieces of Greek art, 2nd rev. ed. Greenwich,
Conn.: New York Graphic Society 1965. Pp.216; 96 color pls.
$17.50 cloth.

These six books, even though they contain excellent illustrations,
are not of the large picture book type in that the texts are fuller
and more discursive. This is especially true for the three by
Charbonneaux, Martin, and Villard in the Arts of Mankind series on
Archaic (13), Classical (14), and Hellenistic (15) Greek art. These
have been translated from the French L'Univers des Formes series.
Charbonneaux writes the sections on sculpture, Martin on architecture,
and Villard on vase painting and the minor arts. The book on
Archaic Greek Art (13) is especially good on the subject of influences
on Greek art and architecture from the Near East and Asia Minor, a
topic which is usually neglected in the handbooks. Perhaps the best
of the three, however, is that on Hellenistic Art (15). It is a
pleasure to find a work which treats in depth all aspects of later
Greek art and architecture. One only wishes that it were in a more
reasonable price range. Demargne's Birth of Greek Art (16) is in
the same Arts of Mankind series (also translated from the French) and
has the same excellent illustrations, but in this case the text is

a little sketchy, especially when it deals with Minoan art and
its influence on Mycenaean Greece. Brilliant (12) tries to compress
the breadth of Greek art into one volume, and, as is typical of
such books, the concentration is on the classical period. The
later Hellenistic period, again, receives short shrift. Chapter
eight, however, on urban architecture and city planning is good.
Unfortunately, Schoder's book (17) can be considered neither good
nor informative. It is basically a pictorial study of Greek art;
the paragraphs of description which accompany the color plates present
little information. The author seems to spend his time exclaiming
over the beauty of his examples rather than explaining their
significance.

(18) HIGGINS, R.A. Greek and Roman jewellery. (Methuen's Handbooks
of Archaeology.) London: Methuen and Co., Ltd. 1961. Pp. 236;
64 monochrome pls.; 4 color pls.; 33 figs. Approx. $13.50 cloth.

(19) RICHTER, G.M.A. Perspective in Greek and Roman art. New York:
Phaidon Publishers, Inc. 1969. Pp. 142; 228 pls. $17.50 cloth.

(20) STRONG, D.E. Greek and Roman gold and silver plate. Ithaca, N.Y.:
Cornell University Press 1966. Pp.235; 68 pls.; 40 figs. $13.50 cloth
These three books survey the minor arts of the Greeks and the Romans.
The title of Higgins' work (18) suggests that it covers both Greek
and Roman jewellery, but in reality it concentrates on Greek. The
Roman section is extremely sketchy and is limited to fifteen pages.
The Etruscan section is also in need of considerable expansion. The
majority of the book, however, on Greek jewellery is excellent;
especially interesting is Part I in which the author discusses the
technical aspects of Greek jewellery. This book is best read in
conjunction with Boardman's Greek Gems and Finger Rings (6).

Strong's work (20) presents a good complement to Higgins' book on jewellery. It deals with all aspects of Greek and Roman gold and silver plate. It is a pleasure to encounter a work in which the Roman part is treated with as much depth as the Greek. Again, the first chapter is especially interesting, for it deals mostly with the ancient craftsman and his techniques. Richter's book (19) is a rather short one for its price, containing only sixty-one pages of text in large print. It is really an essay which grew out of the Appendix to an earlier work, called Furniture of the Greeks and Romans (New York: Phaidon Publishers, Inc. 1966), in which the author discusses ancient perspective as seen in representations of furniture. The present essay expands this appendix to include all aspects of Greek and Roman art. The concentration of the book, however, is on Greek vase painting, from which the majority of illustrative examples are drawn. There are very few examples taken from Roman mural painting, mosaics, or sculpture. There are also few examples from Greek sculpture or from the newly discovered tomb paintings at Paestum. This can be a useful work, if the reader bears in mind its one-sided emphasis on Greek vase painting.

(21) LACY, A.D. Greek pottery in the bronze age. London: Methuen and Co., Ltd. 1967. Pp.303; 115 monochrome pls.; 4 color pls.; 4 maps. Approx. $15.00 cloth.

(22) McDONALD, W.A. and RAPP, G.R., ed. The Minnesota Messenia expedition: reconstructing a bronze age regional environment. Minneapolis: University of Minnesota Press 1972. Pp. 338; 16 pls.; 16 figs.; 11 maps; 14 tables. $22.50 cloth.

(23) MYLONAS, G.E. <u>Mycenae</u> <u>and</u> <u>the</u> <u>Mycenaean</u> <u>age</u>. Princeton: Princeton
University Press 1966. Pp.251; 153 pls.; 26 figs. $27.50 cloth.
Mylonas (23) presents a good survey of Mycenaean Greece, concentrating
on the development of the palace at Mycenae, where he has excavated.
He also treats in some depth other Mycenaean palaces and houses,
such as those at Tiryns and Pylos. This book is best read in
conjunction with Vermeule's <u>Greece</u> <u>in</u> <u>the</u> <u>bronze</u> <u>age</u> (see section III,
p.31). The book edited by McDonald and Rapp (22) is indicative of
the new trends in Greek archaeology, i.e. the multidisciplinary
approach. It attempts to reconstruct the environment of Messenia
during the Bronze Age and includes chapters on surveying and mapping,
soil studies, the agricultural economy, vegetation history, ceramic
studies, metallurgical and geochemical studies, and geophysical
exploration. Every serious student of Greek archaeology should read
this book to learn how the archaeologist can interact and work with
scholars from other disciplines in exploration and excavation. Lacy's
work (21), unfortunately, is rather sketchy for the subject it
attempts to treat. There is a real need for an in depth treatment
of Greek Bronze Age pottery on the same order as Coldstream's <u>Greek</u>
<u>Geometric</u> <u>Pottery</u> (see no.24 below).

(24) COLDSTREAM, J.N. <u>Greek</u> <u>geometric</u> <u>pottery</u>. (Methuen's Handbooks of
Archaeology.) London: Methuen and Co., Ltd. 1968. Pp. 465; 64 pls.
Approx. $32.00 cloth.

(25) DESBOROUGH, V.R.d'A. <u>The</u> <u>Greek</u> <u>dark</u> <u>ages</u>. New York: St. Martin's
Press, Inc. 1972. Pp. 388; 60 pls.; 39 figs. $14.95 cloth.

(26) DESBOROUGH, V.R.d'A. The last Mycenaeans and their successors:
an archaeological survey ca. 1200-1000 B.C. Oxford: Clarendon
Press 1964. Pp. 288; 24 pls. Approx. $18.75 cloth.

(27) SCHWEITZER, B. Greek geometric art. New York: Phaidon Publishers,
Inc. 1971. Pp. 352; 239 pls.; 137 figs. $25.00 cloth.

(28) SNODGRASS, A.M. The dark age of Greece. Chicago: Aldine Publishing
Co. 1971. Pp. 456; 138 ill.; 2 color pls. $20.00 cloth.

The past decade has seen a revival of interest in the Greek Dark Ages,
that period of Greek archaeology and history which begins with the
collapse of Mycenaean civilization (ca. 1150 B.C.) and goes to about
900 B.C. when many regions of Greece embarked upon a period of
expansion and increasing progress. The best overall survey of this
two hundred and fifty year period is Desborough's The Greek Dark Ages
(25). The author treats the evidence by a regional approach,
discussing the development of sites which were important in the
early and late Dark Ages. Especially interesting are the second
and fourth chapters on the early Dark Ages and the material evidence,
respectively. In the second chapter, the author discusses the
various styles of pottery of the early period together with the
contorversial problem of the transition from late Mycenaean to early
Dark Age times. In the fourth chapter, he treats such diverse subjects
as tombs and burial customs, sanctuaries, dress, weapons, and metals.
This book is best read in conjunction with Snodgrass' work (28) of
almost the same name. This is an extremely detailed and exhaustive
synthesis of the available evidence, and for this reason students may
find it hard to read. The most interesting chapter is the fifth, in

which the author discusses the advent of iron into Greece and the
results of the adoption of iron. Students who are interested in the
Greek Dark Ages should read Desborough (25) first for an overall
view and then tackle Snodgrass (28) for an in depth view of the major
problems. Schweitzer (27) presents a more art historical approach.
He discusses developments in the decorative motifs of both Protogeometric and geometric pottery, as well as those of small-scale art,
such as sculpture, tripods, and fibulae. The one area that these books
do neglect, however, is that of architecture. There have been many
developments in this field in the past decade and it is now possible
to write a comprehensive survey of it. Schweitzer does include a brief
chapter on Geometric architecture, but it needs considerable revision
and expansion. Coldstream (24) presents an extremely detailed account
of Protogeometric and Geometric pottery. He concentrates upon the
pottery of Attica, the Argolid, and the Corinthia. His chapters on
Laconian and Western Greek Geometric can now be expanded in the light
of recent discoveries in these areas. Decborough's second book (26)
is a detailed account of the transition from late Mycenaean to early
Dark Age times. Because of its detailed nature, it is not recommended
for general student reading.

(29) BIEBER, M. The history of the Greek and Roman theater, 2nd ed. rev.
Princeton: Princeton University Press 1961. Pp. 343; 866 figs.
$25.00 cloth.

(30) DINSMOOR, W.B. The architecture of ancient Greece. New York: Biblo
and Tannen 1973; New York: Arco Publishing Co., Inc. 1973. Pp. 424;

71 pls.; 125 figs. $27.50 cloth.

First published in 1950.

(31) DREES, L. Olympia: gods, artists and athletes. New York: Praeger 1968. Pp. 193; 82 monochrome pls.; 16 color pls.; 40 figs. $20.00 cloth.

(32) HODGE, A.T. The woodwork of Greek roofs. (Cambridge Classical Studies.) Cambridge: Cambridge University Press 1960. Pp. 150; 16 pls.; 23 figs. Approx. $13.50 cloth.

(33) KARAGEORGHIS, V. Salamis in Cyprus. (New Aspects of Antiquity.) London: Thames and Hudson 1969. Pp. 212; 128 monochrome pls; 17 color pls.; 33 figs. Approx. $13.00 cloth.

Published in the United States as Salamis: recent discoveries in Cyprus. New York: McGraw-Hill 1970. $12.95 cloth.

(34) Thompson, H.A. and Wycherley, R.E. The agora of Athens. (Athenian Agora, vol.14.) Princeton: The American School of Classical Studies at Athens 1972. Pp. 257; 112 pls.; 57 figs. $29.50 cloth.

(35) TRAVLOS, J. Pictorial dictionary of ancient Athens. New York: Praeger 1971. Pp. 590; 722 pls. $70.00 cloth.

Even though Dinsmoor's book (30) was first published in 1950 and is now a little out of date, it is still the best detailed survey of Greek architecture. The original edition has been reprinted both by Biblo and Tannen and by the Arco Publishing Company, but a second revised edition is desperately needed to update not only the text but also the plates, which even in the original edition are fuzzy and lacking in detail. It is best read in conjunction with Hodge's short work on the Woodwork of Greek Roofs (32). Here the author

discusses how wood was used in the superstructure of Greek roofs
by examining four specific examples -- the Temple of Poseidon at
Paestum, the Temple of Hephaestus (Theseion) at Athens, the Megaron
of Demeter at Gaggera, and the Temple of Concord at Agrigento.
Travlos (35) presents an excellent illustrated survey of the topography
and architecture of ancient Athens from Mycenaean times to 300 A.D.
The text and bibliography are detailed. The author describes every
type of building from temple to private house, together with its
sculpture where appropriate. The photographs, drawings, and maps
are all superb. Every student of Classical archaeology should be
familiar with this book, as they should be with the Thompson-
Wycherley survey of the Athenian Agora (34). This latter book is a
synthesis of what is known about the Agora from the American
excavations there during the past forty years. Drees' work (31)
has been translated from the German and is perhaps the best general
work dealing with the sanctuary of Zeus at Olympia. The author
discusses the results of the German excavations at the sanctuary
and presents material which is not found in the usual handbooks;
for example, he examines the workshop of Phidias and the cup with
the inscription on its base reading, "I belong to Phidias." Another
interesting part is the section on the stadium and the judges'
stand in the classical stadium. Karageorghis (33) presents a
synthesis of the results of his excavations at Salamis on Cyprus.
His book purports to deal with Homeric, Hellenistic, and Roman
Salamis, but in reality it concentrates on the Eighth and Seventh
Centuries B.C. and is valuable for its picture of Salamis, and

indeed of all Cyprus, in these two centuries. Bieber's book (29) is the only work in English to present a comprehensive survey of the Greek and Roman theater based on the archaeological evidence. The author discusses the plays of the ancient dramatists in relation to theatrical production, the art of acting, and the buildings themselves.

(36) ADAM, S. The technique of Greek sculpture in the archaic and classical periods. (British School of Archaeology at Athens, supplementary volume no.3.) London: Thames and Hudson 1966. Pp. 137; 72 pls.; 9 figs. Approx. $13.00 cloth.

(37) ASHMOLE, B. Architect and sculptor in classical Greece. New York: New York University Press 1972. Pp. 218; 220 pls. $15.00 cloth.

(38) ASHMOLE, B. and YALOURIS, N. The sculptures of the temple of Zeus. New York: Phaidon Publishers, Inc. 1967. Pp. 188; 211 pls.; 25 figs. $15.00 cloth.

(39) FURTWANGLER, A. Masterpieces of Greek sculpture, new and enlarged ed. Chicago: Argonaut Publishers 1964. Pp. 439; 18 pls.; 87 ill. in text; 177 figs. $20.00 cloth.

First published in German in 1894. First English edition by E. Sellers in 1895. Argonaut edition by A. Oikonomides in 1964.

(40) JENKINS, R.J.H. Dedalica: a study of Dorian plastic art in the seventh century B.C. Washington, D.C.: McGrath Publishing Co. 1971. Pp. 95; 11 pls. $32.00 cloth.

First published in 1936 by Cambridge University Press.

(41) RICHTER, G.M.A. Archaic gravestones of Attica. New York: Phaidon Publishers, Inc. 1961. Pp. 184; 190 figs. $18.50 cloth.

(42) RICHTER, G.M.A. <u>Korai</u>: <u>archaic</u> <u>Greek</u> <u>maidens</u>. New York: Phaidon

Publishers, Inc. 1968. Pp. 327; 689 figs.; 22 pls. $35.00 cloth.

(43) RICHTER, G.M.A. <u>Kouroi</u>: <u>archaic</u> <u>Greek</u> <u>youths</u>, 3rd ed. New York:

Phaidon Publishers, Inc. 1971. Pp. 342; 591 figs. $35.00 cloth.

(44) RICHTER, G.M.A. <u>The</u> <u>portraits</u> <u>of</u> <u>the</u> <u>Greeks</u>, 3 vols. New York:

Phaidon Publishers, Inc. 1965. Pp. 337; 2059 figs. $100.00 cloth.

A supplement to the above three volumes has also been issued,

entitled, <u>The</u> <u>portraits</u> <u>of</u> <u>the</u> <u>Greeks</u>: <u>supplement</u>. New York:

Phaidon Publishers, Inc. 1972. $3.30 paper.

(45) RICHTER, G.M.A. <u>The</u> <u>sculpture</u> <u>and</u> <u>sculptors</u> <u>of</u> <u>the</u> <u>Greeks</u>, 4th ed.

rev. New Haven: Yale University Press 1970. Pp. 317; 853 ill.

$35.00 cloth.

Adolf Furtwängler (39) was really the first to classift Greek

sculptors into schools, and his book, first published in German in

1894, is still a classic in its own right. The first English edition

appeared in 1895. It omitted the chapters on archaic art but included

those on Classical, Fourth Century, and Hellenistic sculpture. This

edition has been reprinted by Argonaut Publishers with the addition

of photographs of works discovered or re-identified since the first

English edition and an updated bibliography. The one drawback to the

1964 English edition is that the photographs in many cases are overly

dark and unclear. The reason for this is that Agronaut have simply

reproduced the plates from the original edition rather than acquiring

new photographs. Richter's <u>Sculpture</u> <u>and</u> <u>Sculptors</u> <u>of</u> <u>the</u> <u>Greeks</u> (45

is perhaps the best general survey in print of Greek sculpture. The

author divides her book into two parts. In the first she discusses

the historical development of Greek sculpture, and in the second

she talks about the individual sculptors and their works. Her
Kouroi (43) and Korai (42) are excellent detailed surveys of the
male and female statues of the sixth and early fifth centuries B.C.
Her Archaic Gravestones of Attica (41) classifies the grave markers
of the same period; and, her Portraits of the Greeks (44) in three
volumes and supplement is an exhaustive treatment of Greek portraiture
of all periods. All the above books by Richter can be used for
student supplementary reading. Jenkins' Dedalica (40) is an
important pioneering work classifying and dating the small scale
sculpture of the Seventh Century B.C. from the Greek mainland. It
is a pleasure to have a reprint of the original 1936 edition; but,
the book really needs to undergo a revision to take into account
recent discoveries. Ashmole's Architect and Sculptor in Classical
Greece (37) is a new work treating the relationship between the
sculpture and the architecture of three major monuments of the Fifth
and Fourth Centuries B.C.: the Temple of Zeus at Olympia, the
Parthenon on the Athenian Acropolis, and the Mausoleum at Halicarnassus.
His Olympia (38) is a detailed study of the sculpture from the
Temple of Zeus at Olympia, discussing new evidence for the placement
of the pedimental figures. It contains excellent photographs. Both
books by Ashmole are highly recommended for supplementary reading.
Adam's Technique of Greek Sculpture (36) is best read after Blumel's
Greek Sculptors at Work (see section IV, p.36). It is quite a
technical book, and students may find it difficult reading.

(46) BIEBER, M. Alexander the Great in Greek and Roman art. Chicago:
Argonaut Publishers 1964. Pp. 98; 63 pls. $7.50 cloth.

(47) BIEBER, M. Copies: contributions to the history of Greek and
Roman art. New York: New York University Press 1973. Pp. 600;
900 ill. $50.00 cloth.

(48) BIEBER, M. Laocoön: the influence of the group since its rediscovery,
2nd ed. Detroit: Wayne State University Press 1967. Pp. 41;
38 figs. $6.95 cloth.

(49) BIEBER, M. The sculpture of the Hellenistic age, rev. ed. New York:
Columbia University Press 1961. Pp. 259; 818 figs. $40.00 cloth.

(50) HAVELOCK, C.M. Hellenistic art. Greenwich, Conn.: New York
Graphic Society, Ltd. 1970. Pp. 283; 177 monochrome pls.;
20 color pls. $18.50 cloth.

These five books constitute the offerings in Hellenistic sculpture.
The best survey of the sculpture of this period, and perhaps the
best survey in any language, is Bieber's Sculpture of the Hellenistic
Age (49). Her book is detailed with an extensive bibliography and
copious photographs. She begins her work with a discussion of the
sculpture of the Fourth Century B.C. and the influence of Lysippus
on Hellenistic sculpture. She then divides her subject into
schools, such as those at Alexandria, Priene, Pergamon, and Rhodes,
and discusses the sculpture from these individual regions. This is
a valid approach, for it serves to bring order to the vast amount
of sculpture belonging to the Hellenistic period. But, the reader
should keep in mind that the Hellenistic period was a cosmopolitan
one with many trends and influences criss-crossing the Mediterranean
and that at times such a neat division of the sculpture into
schools simply cannot be made. In her Copies (47) she examines the
system of copying Greek works of art and discusses the copying
industry which arose in the First Century B.C. Through an examination

of the copying process she attempts to clarify the demarcation
between Greek and Roman sculpture. Her book on <u>Alexander</u> <u>the</u> <u>Great</u>
(46) is an outgrowth of an earlier article entitled, "The Portraits
of Alexander the Great," and published in 1949 in the <u>Proceedings</u>
<u>of</u> <u>the</u> <u>American</u> <u>Philosophical</u> <u>Society</u>. It is an important work
on the history of the Alexander portraits in the Greco-Roman world.
However, the plates (as is so often the case with Argonaut Publishers)
have been badly reproduced. Those of the <u>Laocoön</u> (49) are somewhat
better. This book discusses the Laocoön group, now in the Belvedere
of the Vatican, and its influence since its rediscovery in 1506.
Havelock's <u>Hellenistic</u> <u>Art</u> (50) by its title would lead one to
suppose that it deals with all aspects of Hellenistic art, but in
reality it concentrates on sculpture. Painting, mosaics, and the
minor arts are kept to a bare minimum. The book is really a series
of photographs arranged in chronological order with a brief discussion
attached to each. The text is rather sketchy and needs to be
amplified. The photographs, however, are excellent.

(51) BEAZLEY, J.D. <u>The</u> <u>development</u> <u>of</u> <u>the</u> <u>Attic</u> <u>black-figure</u>. (Sather
    Classical Lectures, vol.24.) Berkeley: University of California
    Press 1964. Pp. 120; 49 pls. $9.50 cloth.

(52) COOK, R.M. <u>Greek</u> <u>painted</u> <u>pottery</u>. (Methuen's Handbooks of
    Archaeology.) London: Methuen and Co., Ltd. 1960. Pp. 395;
    56 pls.; 44 figs. Approx. $15.00 cloth.

(53) L'ORANGE, H.P. and NORDHAGEN, P.J. <u>Mosaics</u> <u>from</u> <u>antiquity</u> <u>to</u> <u>the</u>
    <u>early</u> <u>middle</u> <u>ages</u>. (Methuen's Handbooks of Archaeology.) London:
    Methuen and Co., Ltd. 1966. Pp. 92; 110 pls. Approx. $15.00 cloth.
    First published in 1958.

(54) RICHTER, G.M.A. <u>Attic</u> <u>red-figured</u> <u>vases</u>: <u>a</u> <u>survey</u>, rev. ed.
New Haven: Yale University Press 1958. Pp. 209; 125 figs.
$17.50 cloth.

(55) WEBSTER, T.B.L. <u>Potter</u> <u>and</u> <u>patron</u> <u>in</u> <u>classical</u> <u>Athens</u>. New York:
Barnes and Noble 1972. Pp. 312; 16 pls. $17.50 cloth.

Published in England by Methuen and Co., Ltd.
Even though it is now fifteen years old, Cook's (52) is still the
best general survey in print of Greek painted pottery. He begins
his work with the Protogeometric period and ends with a chapter on
Hellenistic pottery with painted decoration. Also included are
valuable chapters on shapes and techniques. This book is not a
complete work on Greek painted pottery, since it omits both Minoan
and Mycenaean pottery. Nevertheless, it still is an important work.
Beazley's work (51) has now been supplanted to some extent by
Boardman's recent <u>Athenian</u> <u>Black</u> <u>Figure</u> <u>Vases</u> (see section IV, p.37).
It is still important, however, and should be read in conjunction
with Boardman. Richter's book on <u>Attic</u> <u>Red-Figured</u> <u>Vases</u> (54) needs
a slight revision to take into account recent developments and
discoveries, but it is still an important and useful survey, really
the only one of its kind in English. Webster (55) takes a more
historical approach to the subject and examines how potters worked,
who were their patrons, and what types of people bought the decorated
vases. There is a desperate need of a good survey of Greek and
Roman mosaics. The book by L'Orange and Nordhagen is really too
short and sketchy to do justice to this important field. The authors
concentrate on the mosaics from late antiquity and neglect Greek
mosaic decoration. For instance, the pebble mosaics from Olynthus

are only summarily treated; and, there is no discussion of those
from Pella, nor any mention of the problem of where and when the
change from the pebble to the tessera technique took place.

(56) BOARDMAN, J. Archaic Greek gems: schools and artists of the sixth
and early fifth centuries B.C. Evanston, Ill.: Northwestern
University Press 1968. Pp. 236; 40 monochrome pls.; 3 color pls.
$15.00 cloth.

Published in England by Thames and Hudson.

(57) BOARDMAN, J. and KURTZ, D.C. Greek burial customs. Ithaca, N.Y.:
Cornell University Press 1971. Pp. 384; 90 pls.; 92 figs.;
7 maps. $11.50 cloth.

Published in the Aspects of Greek and Roman Life series.

(58) CHARBONNEAUX, J. Greek bronzes. New York: Viking Press 1962.
Pp. 164; 32 pls.; 21 figs. $5.00 cloth.

First published in 1958.

(59) HIGGINS, R.A. Greek terracottas. (Methuen's Handbooks of Archaeology.)
London: Mehtuen and Co., Ltd. 1967. Pp. 169; 64 monochrome pls.;
4 color pls. Approx. $20.00 cloth.

(60) SJÖQVIST, E. Sicily and the Greeks. Ann Arbor: University of
Michigan Press 1973. Pp. 90; 46 figs. $10.00 cloth.

(61) SNODGRASS, A.M. Arms and armour of the Greeks. (Aspects of
Greek and Roman Life series.) Ithaca, N.Y.: Cornell University Press
1967. Pp. 152; 60 pls. $7.50 cloth.

This is a group of six miscellaneous books which do not fit into
any of the above categories. Higgins (59) presents an excellent
survey of Greek terracottas from prehistoric times down to the end
of the Hellenistic period. This is the first book of its kind in
English for a long time and should be valuable to student and

specialist alike. It is well illustrated. That by Charbonneaux
(58) is a short survey of Greek bronze statuettes, including a
good chapter on bronze working. The concentration is on the human
figure; animal figurines, especially of the Geometric period, are
generally neglected, giving a very one-sided aspect to the book.
Boardman (56) gives a detailed catalogue and synthesis of evidence
for Greek gems of the Sixth and early Fifth Centuries B.C. He
brings order to this subject by discerning different hands and
schools at work. For an overall survey of Greek gems, however,
the reader would do better to consult the author's other book (6)
on the subject in which he discusses gems and finger rings from
the early Bronze Age to the late Classical period (end of the Fourth
Century B.C.). One of the most valuable and informative books in
this group is Sjöqvist's <u>Sicily and the Greeks</u> (60). For a
number of years, the author directed the excavations at Morgantina
in Sicily, and in his book he related the history of Morgantina
to the rest of the island. He also synthesizes much of the recent
evidence from the Italian excavations; this information had
previously been tucked away in Italian archaeological periodicals.
He discusses Minoan and Mycenaean contacts with Sicily and the
extent of the Greek colonial penetration inland. It had previously
been thought that the Greeks had confined themselves to the·
coastal areas of Sicily, but Sjöqvist shows that they penetrated
almost to the center of the island. In all, this is perhaps the
most useful book on Greek Sicily in print and is so well written
that it can be used both by the general reader and by the specialist.

Boardman and Kurtz (57) present an excellent survey of Greek

burial customs, concentrating upon Athens and Attica, but also

ranging further afield to other areas of the Greek world. The

authors treat their subject from an archaeological and artistic

approach, rather that from a literary one. For works on the Greek

epitaph, the reader is urged to consult either R. Lattimore, Themes

in Greek and Latin Epitaphs (1942) or C. Clairmont, Gravestone

and Epigram (1970). Especially valuable is the select gazeteer

of cemeteries outside Attica at the back of the book. Snodgrass'

work (61) is in the same "Aspects of Greek and Roman Life" series

as the Boardman-Kurtz book. It is an archaeological and literary

survey of Greek armour and weaponry, well-illustrated.

(62) BANTI, L. The Etruscan cities and their culture. Berkeley:

University of California Press 1973. Pp. 322; 96 pls.;

13 maps. $14.50 cloth.

(63) PALLOTTINO, M. Etruscan painting. New York: Skira Inc.,

Publishers 1952. Pp. 139; 64 color pls. No price listed. Cloth.

Published originally by Skira in Lausanne, Switzerland.

(64) SCULLARD, H.H. The Etruscan cities and Rome. (Aspects of Greek and

Roman Life series.) Ithaca, N.Y.: Cornell University Press 1967.

Pp. 320; 120 pls.; 27 figs. $9.50 cloth.

There are few hardbacks on the subject of Etruscan art and archaeology

that are suitable for the student or the general reader. Banti's

recent work (62) attempts to remedy this situation. It is a general

book dealing with all aspects of the Etruscan world, much in the

same manner as Pallottino's The Etruscans (see section V, p.58).

However, the organization is different, for Banti concentrates
upon the individual cities and their territories. She discusses
the rise and fall of the major cities of both Southern and Northern
Etruria and their commercial and cultural interrelations.
Scullard (64) presents a more historical approach to this topic;
he discusses the growth of the major Etruscan cities together with
that of Rome. Chapter 9 on Etruscan Rome can be useful if read
in conjunction with Bloch's Origins of Rome (see section VII, p.78),
for it updates Bloch's work. The book by Pallottino (63) is
really the only one in English to treat solely the subject of
Etruscan painting, primarily from the tombs at Tarquinia. The
value of this book lies in the color photographs. The reader
must be warned, however, that the colors in the photographs have
been doctored slightly to make them appear more brilliant.

(65) BIANCHI BANDINELLI, R. Rome: center of power 500 B.C.-200 A.D.
(Arts of Mankind series.) New York: George Braziller, Inc.
1970. Pp. 437. $30.00 cloth.

(66) BIANCHI BANDINELLI, R. Rome: the late empire 200-400 A.D.
(Arts of Mankind series.) New York: George Braziller, Inc. 1971.
Pp. 466; 429 ill. $30.00 cloth.

(67) BRILLIANT, R. Roman art: from the Republic to Constantine.
New York: Praeger 1974. Pp. 288; 275 ill.; 11 figs.; 14 plans.
$15.00 cloth, $6.95 paper.

(68) HANFMANN, G.M.A. Roman art: a modern survey of the art of imperial
Rome. Greenwich, Conn.: New York Graphic Society, Ltd. 1964.
145 monochrome pls.; 52 color pls. $20.00 cloth.

The two books by Bianchi Bandinelli (65 and 66) form the Roman
section of the Arts of Mankind series (for the Greek part, see nos.
13, 14, 15, 16), also translated from the French L'Univers des
Formes series. Both are good general surveys with excellent
photographs but have the same failing in that the sections on
architecture are sketchy. The reader would be advised to consult
these books in conjunction with Boëthius and Ward-Perkins' Etruscan
and Roman Architecture (see Appendix 1, p.84), which is the best
treatment of that subject. The book entitled Rome: the Late Empire
(66) is especially valuable for its inclusion of photographs of many
artifacts from the Roman cities of Asia Minor and the Near East.
Both Brilliant (67) and Hanfmann (68) also present general surveys of
Roman art. The paperback edition of Brilliant's book (67) is designed
as a textbook which can be used in undergraduate classes. Hanfmann's
work (68) is basically a pictorial survey, with plates arranged in
chronological order according to subject and a paragraph of
description appended to each. The author concentrates on sculpture
and treats rather sketchily architecture, painting, and mosaics.

(69) MacDONALD, W.L. The architecture of the Roman empire, vol.1: an
introductory study. New Haven: Yale University Press 1965.
Pp. 211; 135 pls.; 10 figs. $17.50 cloth.

(70) MEIGGS, R. Roman Ostia, 2nd ed. Oxford: Clarendon Press 1973.
Pp. 622; 40 pls.; 32 figs.; 1 plan. $27.25 cloth.

(71) NASH, E. Pictorial dictionary of ancient Rome, 2 vols., 2nd rev. ed.
New York: Praeger 1970. Vol.1: Pp. 544; 674 pls. $38.50 cloth.
Vol.2: Pp. 536; 663 pls. $38.50 cloth.

Nash's Dictionary (71) parallels Travlos' Pictorial Dictionary of
Ancient Athens (35) in that it presents a detailed pictorial
survey of the monuments of ancient Rome. This book is highly
recommended, since both text and plates are of a high quality.
MacDonald (69) attempts to treat the problem of interior vs. exterior
space in Roman architecture by examining three major monuments
built between 60 and 130 A.D., i.e. the Palaces of Nero and Domitian,
Trajan's markets by his Forum, and the Pantheon. To some extent,
however, his book has been supplanted by the Boëthius and Ward-Perkins
work on Etruscan and Roman Architecture (see Appendix 1, p.84).
Fortunately, Meiggs' important book on Roman Ostia (70) has gone
through a second edition. It offers a synthesis of the archaeological
and historical evidence on Ostia, presenting in English a synopsis
of the results of the Italian work there.

(72) BRILLIANT, R. Gesture and rank in Roman art. (Memoirs of the
  Connecticut Academy of Arts and Sciences, vol.14, 1963.) New Haven:
  Connecticut Academy of Arts and Sciences 1963. Pp. 238; 479 ill.
  $20.00 paper.

(73) HAMBERG, P.G. Studies in Roman imperial art. Rome: "L'Erma"
  di Bretschneider 1968. Pp. 202; 45 pls.; 7 figs. $20.00 paper.
    First published in 1945.

(74) ROSSI, L. Trajan's column and the Dacian wars. (Aspects of Greek
  and Roman Life series.) Ithaca, N.Y.: Cornell University Press
  1971. Pp. 240; 36 ill.; 157 illustrations of Trajan's column;
  11 figs. $11.50 cloth.

(75) RYBERG, I.S. Panel reliefs of Marcus Aurelius. New York:
Archaeological Institute of America 1967. Pp.102; 63 pls.
$12.00 cloth.

(76) SÄFLUND, G. The Polyphemus and Scylla groups at Sperlonga.
Stockholm: Almqvist and Wiksell 1972. Pp. 116; 70 ill.
Approx. $10.00 paper.

(77) SIMON, E. Ara Pacis Augustae. (Monumenta Artis Antiquae 1.)
Greenwich, Conn.: New York Graphic Society, Ltd. No date.
Pp. 32; 32 pls.; 2 figs. Approx. $10.00 cloth.

(78) STRONG, E. Roman sculpture from Augustus to Constantine.
New York: Arno Press 1971. Pp. 408; 130 pls. $25.00 cloth.
First published in 1907.

(79) VOGEL, L. The column of Antoninus Pius. (Loeb Classical
Monographs.) Cambridge: Harvard University Press 1973. Pp. 220;
99 ill. $16.00 cloth.

The above eight books all deal with certain aspects of Roman
sculpture. Still the best survey of this subject is Strong's
work (78) which was first published in 1907 and has been reprinted
twice in recent years. It is really the only book in English to
present a detailed account of the development of Roman sculpture but
needs to be reissued in a revised edition that takes into account
new discoveries and theories. There are, however, several good
works on individual monuments. For instance, Erika Simon's
monograph (77) on the Augustan altar of peace (13-9 B.C.) is
excellent, as are those by Rossi (74) and Vogel (79) on the columns
of Trajan and Antoninus Pius, respectively. Both latter works
present detailed analyses of the sculpture of these columns with

copious comparative material. That by Rossi (74) in the excellent
"Aspects of Greek and Roman Life" series published by Cornell
University Press has been translated from the Italian by Jocelyn
Toynbee. The only problem with this book is that some of the
photographs of the spirals from Trajan's column are a little
overexposed. Vogel (79) presents a comprehensive account of the
column of Antoninus Pius, the remains of which include the
decorated pedestal, four fragments of the pedestal reliefs, and
the bottom of the red granite shaft. Similarly, the monographs
by Ryberg (75) and Säflund (76) deal with the sculpture of individual
monuments. Säflund has spent many years working on the reconstruction
of the sculptures (from the story of the Odyssey) from the Tiberian
cave at Sperlonga and presents here a report on two of the better
preserved groups. Hamberg's Studies in Roman Imperial Art (73)
has been reprinted from the original 1945 edition. It is a
welcome reprint, since the book treats an important contribution of
the Romans to sculpture, that of the historical and allegorical
narrative. Especially interesting are the third and fourth chapters,
dealing with the epic/documentary tradition in state reliefs and
the relationship between convention and realism in battle scenes,
respectively. Brilliant's monograph (72) treats the importance of
the gesture in Roman imperial sculpture and coinage. It is perhaps
best read in conjunction with Hamberg's Studies (73). Both books
together illustrate the importance of the historical event in Roman
art, especially sculpture.

(80) DORIGO, W. Late Roman painting: a study of pictorial records.
New York: Praeger 1971. Pp. 345; 222 pls.; 6 maps. $35.00 cloth.

(81) MAIURI, A. Roman painting. New York: Skira Inc., Publishers 1952.
Pp. 155; 84 color pls. No price listed. Cloth.

(82) PETERS, W.J.T. Landscape in Romano-Campanian mural painting.
Assen: Koninklijke van Gorcum & Co. 1963. Pp. 240; 47 pls.
No price listed. Paper.

(83) WEITZMANN, K. Ancient book illumination. (Martin Classical
Lectures, vol.XVI.) Cambridge: Harvard University Press 1959.
Pp. 166; 64 pls. $10.00 cloth.

The above four books deal with the area of Roman painting. Peters
(82) concentrates upon another important element in Roman art, that
of the landscape and of the portrayal of the human figure in its
proper perspective in relation to the surrounding landscape.
Maiuri's work (81) is really the only one in English to treat
in general manner the vast subject of Roman painting. Yet, it
has the same weakness as Pallottino's Etruscan Painting (63),
also published by Skira Inc., a firm which is based in Lausanne,
Switzerland. The colors of the photographs have been doctored
to make them appear brighter than they really are. Dorigo (80)
discusses all types of painted decoration from the First Century B.C.
to the Sixth Century A.D., including mosaics, inlays, manuscript
illustrations, designs on textiles, as well as painted panels.
Kurt Weitzmann (83) has done pioneering work in the field of
ancient manuscript illumination. In an earlier work entitled,
Illustrations in Roll and Codex (Princeton: Princeton University

Press 1947), which has fortunately been reissued by Princeton
University Press, he proved the existence of manuscript
illumination in classical antiquity. In this subsequent book,
he synthesizes the evidence for the different types of illustrations,
examining those from ancient scientific treatises, epic poetry,
dramatic poetry, and literary prose texts. This book is highly
recommended for supplementary reading in an extremely interesting
field.

(84) CHARLESTON, R.J. Roman pottery. New York: Pitman Publishing
Corporation. No date. Pp. 48; 96 monochrome pls.; 4 color pls.
$17.50 cloth.

(85) HAYES, J.W. Late Roman pottery. London: The British School at
Rome 1972. Pp. 477; 23 pls.; 93 figs.; 40 maps. Approx. $20.00 cloth.
These two books on Roman pottery present two extremes. That by
Charleston (84) is a very sketchy account of the different types
of pottery extant in the Roman world. On the other hand, Hayes
(85) gives an extremely detailed and thorough account of late Roman
pottery. What is needed is a survey of Roman pottery of all types
and periods, much along the same lines as Coldstream's pioneering
work on Greek Geometric Pottery (24).

(86) BREGLIA, L. Roman imperial coins: their art and technique.
New York: Praeger 1968. Pp. 236; 99 pls. Approx. $20.00 cloth.

(87) GALINSKY, G.K. Aeneas, Sicily and Rome. (Monographs in Art and
Archaeology, vol.40.) Princeton: Princeton University Press 1969.
Pp. 278; 173 ill.; 6 figs. $13.50 cloth.

(88) TOYNBEE, J.M.C. Art in Roman Britain, 2nd ed. Los Angeles:
Hennessey and Ingalls, Inc. 1962. Pp. 219; 230 ill. $15.00 cloth.

This is a group of three miscellaneous books that do not fit into
any of the previous categories on Roman art. Breglia's work
(86) has been translated from the Italian L'arte romana nelle monete
dell' età imperiale and is a pictorial history of the art on
Roman imperial coins. After a short introduction of thirty-two
pages are 99 plates followed by a secyion of commentary for each
one. The book is valuable for its plates and for the rather full
commentary on them. Galinsky (87) has written an interesting book
on the Trojan legend (and its background) about the coming of Aeneas
to Italy. Finally, Toynbee's Art in Roman Britain (88) is another
pictorial presentation (with a short introduction of seventeen
pages). The book covers material that will be unfamiliar to
American readers, i.e. the sculpture, fresco painting, mosaics,
decorated armor, metalwork, and glass of Roman Britain.

In addition to the above works by individual authors, there have been
issued reports on the results of excavations at various sites. Perhaps
the two most important American sites are those at the Athenian Agora
and at Corinth. In both cases, the excavations have been carried out
by the American School of Classical Studies at Athens. Seventeen
volumes (out of a probable twenty) of results from the Agora have
already been published; sixteen volumes of Corinth excavations have
been published; and, work is still continuing in these areas.
In the Sanctuary of the Great Gods on the island of Samothrace,
excavations have been conducted by the Institute of Fine Arts, New
York University, and the American School at Athens. Four volumes
(out of a probable nine) of results have been issued. The excavations
carried out under the late Carl Blegen at the Palace of Nestor at Pylos

have been completed and three volumes have been published, entitled
The Palace of Nestor at Pylos in Western Messenia (1966-1973).
Perhaps the most important British site is that of the Palace of
Minos at Knossos. Work began here under Sir Arthur Evans and is still
in progress. Evans' final publication, entitled The Palace of Minos
at Knossos, in four volumes was first issued between 1921-1935. It
has recently (1963) been reprinted, as has been his Knossos Fresco
Atlas (1967). Other work by the British School of Archaeology in
Athens has been carried out at the Sanctuaries of Hera Akraia and
Limenia at Perachora. The first volume by Humfry Payne, published
in 1940, has long been out of print, but the second volume on the
pottery, ivories, and scarabs, edited by T.J. Dunbabin, is still in
print.

Preliminary progress reports and results of smaller American and
British excavations are published in the journals of the archaeological
schools, i.e. Hesperia, the journal of the American School of Classical
Studies at Athens, and the Annual of the British School of Archaeology.
For results of excavations conducted in Italy, the reader should
consult the Memoirs of the American Academy at Rome. The American
Journal of Archaeology, published by the Archaeological Institute
of America, contains not only excavation reports but also articles on
sculpture, painting, etc., as well as book reviews. Two British
periodicals, the Journal of Hellenic Studies and the Journal of Roman
Studies, published by the Societies for the Promotion of Hellenic and
Roman Studies, respectively, present articles of both an archaeological
and an historical nature.

Finally, mention should be made of the Corpus Vasorum Antiquorum, begun in 1922. It represents an attempt to provide photographs and descriptions of Greek and Roman vases in European and American museums. To date, twelve fasicules of vases from American museums and thirteen from British museums have been published.

APPENDIX (NO.3) ON FRENCH AND GERMAN BOOKS.

This appendix comprises a select list of French and German books
which may be of use to the student and to the general reader.
Unless otherwise stated, all the books are hardcover editions.
Due to the fluctuation of the value of the dollar, no prices have
been listed, since they change so frequently. However, all the books
listed in this appendix are above the $10.00 limit imposed in the
main part of this bibliography. Again, for the sake of conciseness,
books will be discussed in groups.

(1) CURTIUS, L. Die antike kunst: die klassische kunst Griechenlands,
2nd ed. Darmstadt: Wissenschaftliche Buchgesellschaft 1959.
Pp. 466; 36 pls.; 604 figs.

First published in 1938.

(2) WINCKELMANN, J.J. Geschichte der kunst altertums. Darmstadt:
Wissenschaftliche Buchgesellschaft 1972. Pp. 423; 123 ill. Paper.

First published in 1764.

These two books have recently been reprinted. All students of
ancient art should be familiar with the contents of Winckelmann's
monumental treatise (2), which was first published in 1764.
Winckelmann was the first to write a major work on Greek art and was
responsible for focussing attention on Greek sculpture and for
causing an awakening of interest in this area. Curtius' book (1),
although more recent (1938), is yet no less important, for it is
one of the best surveys of Greek art in any language.

(3) MATZ, F., ed. Die antiken sarcophagreliefs, 5 vols. Berlin:
Gebr. Mann Verlag 1952-1969.

(4) SCHEFOLD, K. Die Griechen und ihre nachbarn. (Propyläen
Kunstgeschichte, vol.1.) Berlin: Propyläen Verlag 1967. Pp. 373;
432 pls.; 74 figs.

(5) SCHEFOLD, K. Meisterwerke griechischer kunst. Basel-Stuttgart:
Benno Schwabe & Co. Verlag 1960. Pp. 320; 743 ill.

(6) SCHUCHHARDT, W.-H., ed. Die antike plastik, 12 vols. Berlin:
Gebr. Mann Verlag 1962 --.

The two books by Karl Schefold (4 and 5) are in effect pictorial
histories of Greek art, both containing some of the best photographs
available anywhere. His Greeks and their Neighbors (4) is
especially interesting in that it concentrates on the relationships
of the Greeks with their neighbors to the east and the west and
contains illustrations of material from these areas. Schuchhardt
has edited a series entitled Die antike Plastik (6) which has now
reached 12 volumes. The volumes each contain a series of essays
on sculptures recently acquired by American and European museums
or found in excavations. It is really an updating of such previous
collections of sculpture as Brunn-Bruckmann, Denkmäler griechischer
und römischer Skulptur, or Arndt-Amelung-Lippold, Photographische
Einzelaufnahmen antiker Skulpturen. Matz (3) has edited a
similar series on decorated sarcophagi. His work can be divided into
three parts, dealing with sarcophagi containing Dionysiac scenes,
representations of the Muses, and later Etruscan stone sarcophagi,
respectively.

(7) BRUNEAU, P. and DUCAT, J. Guide de Délos. (École Francaise d'Athenes.) Paris: E. de Boccard 1965. Pp. 175; 24 pls.; 37 figs.

(8) DAUX, G. Guide de Thasos. (École Française d'Athènes.) Paris: E. de Boccard 1968. Pp. 214; 5 pls.; 116 figs.

(9) HELBIG, W. Führer durch die öffentlichen sammlungen klassischer altertümer in Rom, 4th ed. prepared by H. Speier, 4 vols. Tübingen: Verlag Ernst Wasmuth 1963-1972.

    Vol. 1: 1963. Pp. 844.
    Vol. 2: 1966. Pp. 910.
    Vol. 3: 1969. Pp. 875.
    Vol. 4: 1972. Pp. 658.

(10) KIRSTEN, E. and KRAIKER, W. Griechenlandkunde: ein führer zu klassischen stätten, 5th ed., 2 vols. Heidelberg: Carl Winter Universitätsverlag 1967. Pp. 935; 24 pls.; 193 figs.

(11) MATTON, L. and R. Athènes et ses monuments. Athens: Institut Français d'Athènes 1963. Pp. 152; 259 pls.; 27 figs. Paper.

(12) TIRÉ, C. and EFFENTERRE, H. van. Guide des fouilles en Crète. (École Française d'Athènes.) Paris: E. de Boccard 1966. Pp. 111; 24 pls.; 27 figs.

(13) TÖLLE, R. Die anitke stadt Samos. Mainz am Rhein: Verlag Philipp von Zabern 1969. Pp. 123; 68 ill.

This section consists of guide books to various excavations and museums in Greece and Rome. That by Kirsten-Kraiker is perhaps the best archaeological guide to Greece in any language. It is detailed and is limited to archaeological information only. For travel information, the reader should consult the Blue Guide to Greece, edited by Stuart Rossiter. The fifth edition (10) covers new

finds up to 1965. The three guides sponsored by the Ecole Francaise
d'Athenes on its excavations on Crete (12), Delos (7), and Thasos (8)
are all excellent and useful, as is the small German guide to the
ancient city of Samos (13). Lya and Raymond Matton (11) have written
a rather unusual book on the monuments of Athens. They do not
treat Ancient Athens but begin their work with the buildings of the
Seventeenth Century. Many of the monuments existing at that time,
of course, belonged to the Greco-Roman period, and we get a glimpse
of how these ancient monuments survived through Turkish rule.
The monumental guide by Helbig (9) to the Greek and Roman statuary
in the various museums in Rome has been updated in a new edition
by Hermine Speier. This valuable work collects together and
discusses all the examples of Greek and Roman sculpture in the
Roman museums. Each entry contains remarks on identification,
style, and dating with updated bibliography.

(14) COURBIN, P. La céramique géométrique de l'Argolide, 2 vols.
    Paris: E. de Boccard 1966. Pp. 595; 152 pls. Paper.

(15) DRERUP, H. Griechische baukunst in geometrischer zeit.
    (Archaeologia Homerica II, O.) Göttingen: Vandenhoeck & Ruprecht
    1969. Pp. 136; 8 pls.; 59 figs. Paper.

(16) SINOS, S. Die vorklassischen hausformen in der Ägäis. Mainz am
    Rhein: Verlag Philipp von Zabern 1971. Pp. 124; 119 pls.
    Sinos (16) sttempts to present a survey of Bronze Age and early Iron
    Age architecture in the Aegean. A book of this type has long been
    needed, especially one that treats domestic architecture along with
    the palaces and examines both the continuation of traditions and

the influx of new ideas in the early Iron Age. Unfortunately,
Sinos' book appears to be a compendium of results taken from
individual excavation reports. A considerable number of excavations
were conducted during the first part of this century and, in the
light of new evidence, their results need reexamination. If
Sinos had done this and had presented new interpretations of the
evidence, then his book would have been a valuable one. But, as
it is, he repeats old ideas; this is especially true for his
section on the early Iron Age. For instance, the material from
Thermon needs considerable reexamination. This same criticism
can be applied to Drerup's treatise (15). There is need for a
book on Geometric architecture which reexamines the old evidence
and incorporates the new evidence which has come to light within
the past decade. Finally, Courbin (14) presents a comprehensive
account of Geometric pottery from the Argolid.

(17) BAELEN, J. La chronique du Parthénon. Paris: Société
d'Édition "Les Belles Lettres" 1956. Pp. 160; 43 ill. Paper.
(18) BÜSING, H.H. Die griechische halbsaüle. Wiesbaden: Franz Steiner
Verlag 1970. Pp. 87; 8 pls.; 78 figs.
(19) MARTIN, R. Manuel d'architecture grecque, vol.1. Paris: Éditions
A. et J. Picard 1965. Pp. 522; 56 pls.; 223 figs. Paper.
(20) RICHARD, H. Vom ursprung des dorischen temples. Bonn: Rudolf
Habelt 1970. Pp. 60; 25 figs. Paper.
One of the best books on Greek architecture is that by Martin (19).
it is an exhaustive treatment of materials and techniques, subjects
which usually receive sketchy treatment in books on Greek architecture.

It is, therefore, a valuable and informative book. The proposed
second and third volumes on styles and plans, respectively,
have not yet appeared, but the author's intention here is to
discuss the physical remains. Richard's book on the origins of the
Doric temple (20) is rather short and sketchy. For instance, the
author does not treat with sufficient depth the importance of
the temples and shrines of the geometric period nor does he discuss
in what ways they developed into the classical temple plan. The
same criticism can be applied to Büsing's work (18). The text is
sketchy and generally uninformative. Baelen's book (17) is best read
in conjunction with L. and R. Matton, Athènes et ses monuments (11),
since it recounts the history of the Parthenon and the Athenian
Acropolis not only in Classical times but also in Roman, Byzantine,
Turkish, and modern times.

(21) BERGER, E. Das Basler arztrelief. Basel: Archäologischer Verlag
1970. Pp. 202; 167 ill.

(22) BROMMER, F. Die metopen des Parthenon, 2 vols. Mainz am Rhein:
Verlag Philipp von Zabern 1967. Pp. 247; 244 pls.; 19 figs.

(23) BROMMER, F. Die skulpturen der Parthenon-giebel, 2 vols. Mainz
am Rhein: Verlag Philipp von Zabern 1963. Pp. 180; 152 pls.; 15 figs.

(24) BUSCHOR, E. Frühgriechische jünglinge. Munich: R. Piper & Co.
Verlag 1950. Pp. 160; 180 ill.

(25) DIEPOLDER, H. Die attischen grabreliefs des 5. und 4. jahrhunderts
v. Chr. Darmstadt: Wissenschaftliche Buchgesellschaft 1965.
Pp. 64; 54 pls.
    First published in 1931.

(26) KÄHLER, H. Das griechische metopenbild. Munich: F. Bruckmann

Verlag 1949. Pp. 112; 95 pls.; 22 figs.

(27) KAROUZOS, CH. Aristodikos. Stuttgart: W. Kohlhammer Verlag 1961.

Pp. 95; 16 pls. Paper.

(28) LIPPOLD, G. Die griechische plastik. (Handbuch der Altertums-

wissenschaft, vol.6, part 3.) Munich: C.H. Beck'sche

Verlagsbuchhandlung 1950. Pp. 441; 136 pls.

(29) MÖBIUS, H. Die ornamente der griechischen grabstelen, 2nd ed.

Munich: Wilhelm Fink Verlag 1968. Pp. 125; 72 pls.

(30) SCHLÖRB, B. Untersuchungen zur bildhauergeneration nach Phidias.

Waldsassen/Bayern: Stiftland Verlag KG. 1964. Pp. 78; 11 pls. Paper.

The above ten works constitute an excellent selection in German

on Classical Greek sculpture. Perhaps the best and most detailed

survey of Greek sculpture in one volume is Lippold's Die griechische

Plastik (28). One general criticism, however, is that the rather

short and sketchy section on Geometric and Orientalizing sculpture

needs to be expanded, especially in the light of recent discoveries.

For a fuller treatment of geometric sculpture, the reader should

consult Schweitzer, Greek Geometric Art (Appendix 2, no.27). Even

though Kähler's book on Greek metope decoration (26) was published

in 1949, it is still the only thorough work to treat solely the

development of metope sculpture. Buschor's work (24) has to some

extent been supplanted by Richter's Kouroi (Appendix 2, no.43). Yet,

both books should be consulted for a comprehensive picture of archaic

Greek free-standing sculpture. Karouzos (27) discusses not only

works that can be attributed to the sculptor, Aristodikos, but also

treats in general late archaic Attic sculpture and grave statues.
Brommer's two works on the metope (22) and pedimental (23) sculpture
from the Parthenon are definitive; in each one the author presents
a catalogue of the sculptures and associated fragments and reconstructs
the placement of the figures. Schlörb (30) treats the generation of
sculptors after Phidias, concentrating on Alkamenes, Agorakritos,
and Callimachus. In all, the author presents a good survey of
the Athenian sculptors immediately after Phidias. Even though
Diepolder's book was first published in 1931, it (25) is still an
excellent survey of the Attic grave reliefs of the Fifth and Fourth
Centuries B.C. It makes an excellent complement to Richter's
Archaic Gravestones of Attica (Appendix 2, no.41) and is best read
in conjunction with Möbius' Ornaments of Greek Grave Stelai (29)
which discusses the development of the finial, that part of the grave
stele which sits on top of the rectangular marker. A most interesting
book is that by Berger (21) which treats Greek grave and votive
reliefs of the late archaic period with an Hippocratic subject-
matter, i.e. reliefs of medicine and healing. This is really the
only such book in **any** language.

(31) BERNOULLI, J.J. Griechische ikonographie, 3 vols. Hildesheim:
Georg Olms Verlagsbuchhandlung 1969.

    Vol.1: Pp. 215; 26 pls.; 37 figs. First published in 1901.
    Vol.2: Pp. 241; 33 pls.; 22 figs. First published in 1901.
    Vol.3: Pp. 156; 9 pls.; 40 figs. First published in 1905.

(32) BUSCHOR, E. Das hellenistische bildnis. Munich: Biederstein
Verlag 1949. Pp. 70; 62 figs.

(33) PICARD, CH. Manuel d'archéologie grecque: la sculpture - periode

classique, IVe siècle. Paris: A. Picard 1966.

> Vol.1 (2 parts): 12 pls.; 395 ill. On the youthful Praxiteles & Sco
> Vol.2,1: 10 pls.; 177 ill. On Scopas (ctd.) and the older Praxitele
> Vol.2,2: 22 pls.; 382 ill. On Lysippus and Leochares.

(34) SCHOBER, A. Die kunst von Pergamon. Innsbruck-Wien: Margarete
Friedrich Rohrer Verlag 1951. Pp. 202; 161 ill.

(35) STÄHLER, K.P. Das unklassisches im Telephosfries. Munster Westf.
Aschendorfsche Verlagsbuchhandlung 1966. Pp. 216; 24 pls.
The above five books are excellent in the field of Fourth Century
and Hellenistic sculpture. Picard (33) presents an exhaustive
treatment in four volumes on the sculpture of the Fourth Century
B.C., concentrating on the four major sculptors of the period,
Praxiteles, Scopas, Lysippus, and Leochares. Two earlier volumes
on the archaic and classical periods, published in 1935 and 1939,
respectively, are now out of print. Bernoulli's monumental
work (31), first published in 1901-5, is the first thorough study of
Greek portraiture. It has been supplanted to some extent by
Richter's Portraits of the Greeks (Appendix 2, no.44) but still
bears reading. The third volume in the form of an addendum is
really a treatise on the portraits of Alexander the Great. It is
a much fuller treatment of the subject that Bieber's Alexander the
Great in Greek and Roman Art (Appendix 2, no. 46) and should be
read in conjunction with it. Buschor's book (32) treats
specifically Hellenistic portraiture and is valuable because the
author examines the influence that Greek portraiture exerted over
the Roman portraits of the late Republic and early Empire. Schober's
work (34) is extremely valuable because it is the only work in

any language to examine in detail the sculpture from Pergamon,
which produced one of the most important sculptural schools of
the Hellenistic period. The plates, however, in some cases
have been badly reproduced, being either quite dark or very
unclear. More specifically, Stähler (35) treats the Telephos
frieze on the interior wall of the great altar to Zeus at Pergamon
and emphasizes the characteristics in this frieze which foreshadow
many features of Roman narrative sculpture.

(36) BRUNEAU, P. Les mosaiques. (École Française d'Athènes, Exploration
Archéologique de Délos.) Paris: École Francaise 1973. Pp. 332.

(37) KRAIKER, W. Die Malerei der Griechen. Stuttgart: W. Kohlhammer
Verlag 1958. Pp. 166; 76 monochrome pls.; 6 color pls.

(38) OVERBECK, J. Die antiken schriftquellen zur geschichte der bildenden
künste bei den Griechen. Hildesheim: Georg Olms Verlagsbuchhandlung
1959. Pp. 488.

First published in Leipzig in 1868.

(39) ROHDE, E. Griechische terrakotten. (Monumenta Artis Antiquae 4.)
Tübingen: Ernst Wasmuth Verlag. No date. Pp. 52; 36 monochrome
pls.; 12 color pls.

The above four books are a miscellaneous grouping on various aspects
of Greek art. Kraiker's book (37) on Greek painting has the same
defects that so many such works have in that it concentrates on vase
painting and neglects the various painted tombs and grave stelai
that represent important evidence for Hellenistic painting.
Bruneau (36) has written an important new work on mosaics, but he
concentrates on those found on Delos. One really needs a thorough

examination of all known Greek mosaics; there is now enough
evidence for a large scale work on this subject. Rohde's work (39)
is rather short and sketchy; the reader would do better to consult
Higgins' book on the subject (Appendix 2, no.59). Fortunately,
Overbeck's important book (38) has been reprinted. It is a
compilation of all the ancient sources on sculpture and painting.
It is a much fuller treatment of the subject than either of
Pollitt's two books (see section IV, pp.51, 53), but needs to
undergo a revision to take into account evidence from inscriptions
and papyri accumulated during the past hundred years.

(40) HAMPE, R. and SIMON, E. Griechische sagen in der frühen
    Etruskischen kunst. Mainz am Rhein: Verlag Philipp von Zabern
    1964. Pp. 71; 30 pls.; 12 figs.

(41) HERBIG, R. Götter und dämonen der Etrusker, 2nd ed. prepared by
    E. Simon. Mainz am Rhein: Verlag Philipp von Zabern 1965.
    Pp. 51; 50 pls.; 10 figs.

    First published in 1948.

Both works listed above deal with the same basic subject-matter.
Herbig's book on Gods and Demons of the Etruscans (41), first
published in 1948, has been revised by Erika Simon. It is an
important book for understanding the demonology of the Etruscans.
The work by Hampe and Simon (40) examines the influence of Greek
mythology on early Etruscan art. The authors, unfortunately,
concentrate on vase painting and largely neglect other media of
artistic expression. Yet, despite the above reservation, this
book is important, for it emphasizes the amount of influence the Greeks
had on Etruscan art.

(42) KÄHLER, H. Rom und seine welt: bilder zur geschichte und kultur,

2 vols. Munich: Bayerischer Schulbuch Verlag 1958-60.

Vol. of text: Pp. 487; 149 figs.
Vol. of plates: Pp. 44; 288 pls.; 9 figs.

(43) KRAUS, T. Das Römische weltreich. (Propyläen Kunstgeschichte, vol.2.)

Berlin: Propyläen Verlag 1967. Pp. 336; 416 pls.; 46 figs.

(44) LÜBKE-PERNICE, Die kunst der Römer, rev. ed. prepared by B. Sarne.

Wien-Berlin-Stuttgart: Paul Neff Verlag 1958. Pp. 456; 420 ill.;

8 color pls.

In general, the works on Roman art and archaeology are meager in

comparison with the offerings on the Greek side. The two books

by Kähler (42) and Kraus (43) are pictorial histories of Roman art

and architecture with excellent photographs. Kähler (42) provides

a separate volume of plates. Kraus' work (43) is a little shorter.

Unfortunately, the author begins with the Second Century B.C. and

omits the development of Rome in the early centuries of its

existence. Sarne has revised the hundred year old Lübke-Pernice

work (44) on Roman art and has included the latest material (up to

1958) on pre-urban and Etruscan Rome. For general information, the

reader would be advised to consult the Sarne revision for early

Rome and then switch to either Kraus or Kähler for late Republican

and Imperial Rome.

(45) CURTIUS, L. Das antike Rom, 4th ed. Vienna-Munich: Verlag

Anton Schroll & Co. 1963. Pp. 216; 186 pls.; 3 plans.

First published in 1944.

(46) KÄHLER, H. Der römische tempel. Berlin: Gebr. Mann Verlag 1970.

Pp. 42; 72 pls.; 27 figs.

(47) ZANKER, P. Forum Augustum: das bildprogramm. (Monumenta Artis Antiquae 2.) Tübingen: Ernst Wasmuth Verlag. No date. Pp. 32; 40 pls.; 4 figs.

(48) ZANKER, P. Forum Romanum. (Monumenta Artis Antiquae 5.) Tübingen: Ernst Wasmuth Verlag. No date. Pp. 57; 34 pls. Curtius' Ancient Rome (45) is really the poor man's equivalent to Nash's Pictorial Dictionary of Ancient Rome (Appendix 2, no.71). It attempts to do the same thing but limits itself to one volume. In fact, Nash was responsible for preparing the new fourth edition. Both text and plates are excellent and make the book well worth reading. Kähler's short book (46) on the Roman temple is more in the nature of a pictorial survey with copious good photographs. For a full treatment of this subject, the reader should consult Boethius and Ward-Perkins, Etruscan and Roman Architecture Appendix 1, p.84). The two small books by Zanker on the building programs in the Augustan Forum (47) and the Roman Forum (48) are in the same Monumenta Artis Antiquae series. They both present a general picture of the types of buildings and their history in these fora in Rome.

(49) BERNOULLI, J.J. Römische ikonographie, 2 vols. Hildesheim: Georg Olms 1969.

Vol.1: Pp. 305; 29 pls.; 43 figs. First published in 1882.
Vol.2: Pp. 438; 35 pls.; 59 figs. First published in 1886.

(50) SCHMIDT, M. Der Basler Medeasarkophag. (Monumenta Artis Antiquae 3.) Tübingen: Ernst Wasmuth Verlag. No date. Pp. 40; 32 pls. Bernoulli's work on Roman portraits (49) first published in 1882-6 is a companion work to his volumes on Greek portraiture (31).

L i k e the Greek work, it is a little out of date but still is one of the very few works to treat the whole range of Roman portraiture. Schmidt's short book (50) on the Medea sarchopagus in Basel discusses sarcophagi in general (in the way of comparative material) and is thus a good survey of this type of decoration.

(51) CURTIUS, L. Die wandmalerei Pompejis. Darmstadt: Wissenschaftliche Buchgesellschaft 1960. Pp. 472; 226 ill.; 12 color pls.

First published in 1929.

(52) SCHEFOLD, K. Vergessenes Pompeji. Bonn-Munich: Francke Verlag 1962. Pp. 218; 164 monochrome pls.; 16 color pls.

(53) SCHEFOLD, K. Die wände Pompejis. Berlin: Walter de Gruyter & Co. 1957. Pp. 378.

Even though Curtius' book (51) on Pompeian wall painting was first published in 1929, it still remains a classic in its own right and deserves to be read by all students of Roman art and archaeology. Schefold's Vergessenes Pompejis (52) is important for it brings to light unusual and little known paintings from Pompeii. His other work on the walls of Pompeii (53) is a register of the locations and state of preservation of all the paintings discovered through the years at Pompeii. It is thus extremely usefyl as a reference book.

In addition to the above individual works, the following German excavation reports are of note:

(1) **BAALBEK.** Results of excavations in the years 1898-1905, ed. T. Wiegand. 3 vols. in 4.

(2) GERMANY. Römisch-Germanische Forschungen, 36 vols. 1928 --.

Still in progress; latest volume published in 1975.

(3) KABIRION. Das Kabirenheiligtum bei Theben, 7 vols. 1940 --.

Vol.1: Das Kabirenheiligtum bei Theben. 1940.
Vols.2-4: in preparation.
Vol.5: B. Schmaltz, Terrakotten aus dem Kabirenheiligtum bei Theben. 197
Vols.6-7: in preparation.

(4) KERAMEIKOS, ATHENS. Kerameikos. Ergebnisse der Ausgrabungen, 13 vols.

1940 --. Still in progress; latest volume published in 1975.

(5) MILETUS. Milet. Ergebnisse der Ausgrabungen und Untersuchungen seit

dem Jahre 1899, 4 vols. 1906 --.

Vol.1, 9 fasicules.
Vol.2, 4 fasicules.
Vol.3, 5 fasicules.
Vol.4, 2 fasicules.

In addition to the above, a supplement in the nature of a guide book

has been issued:

G. Kleiner, Die Ruinen von Milet. Berlin: Walter de Gruyter 1968.

Pp. 164; 120 ill.; 1 plan. Approx. $12.00 cloth.

(6) OLYMPIA. Berichte über die Ausgrabungen in Olympia, 8 vols., ed.

Emil Kunze. 1937-67.

(7) OLYMPIA. Olympische Forschungen, 8 vols., ed. E. Kunze. 1944 --. Stil

progress; latest volume published in 1975.

(8) PERGAMON. Altertümer von Pergamon, 11 vols. 1885 --. This series

of excavation reports has now reached 11 volumes, the first published

in 1885 and the most recent in 1975. The series is now edited by

Erich Boehringer.

(9). PERGAMON. Pergamenische Forschungen, 2 vols., ed. E. Boehringer.

Vol.1: Pergamon: Gesammelte Aufsätze. 1972.
Vol.2: J. Schäfer, Hellenistische Keramik aus Pergamon. 1968.

(10) SPAIN. Madrider Forschungen, 11 vols. 1956 --. Still in
    progress; latest volume issued in 1975.

The major German archaeological periodical is the Jahrbuch des Deutschen
Archäologischen Instituts, published by the German Archaeological
Institute. This journal contains articles on Greek and Roman architecture,
sculpture, painting, etc. Notices of excavation results are published
in the Archäologischer Anzeiger which is issued once a year and is usually
bound by libraries at the end of the appropriate Jahrbuch. The German
Archaeological Institute also publishes an Archäologische Bibliographie,
the latest of which appeared in 1974.
There are also 25 supplementary volumes on individual topics. These are
called the Ergänzungshefte zum Jahrbuch des Deutschen Archäologischen
Instituts.
The schools of the German Archaeological Institute in the various
Mediterranean countries also issue their own journals. These are:
   ATHENS. Mitteilungen des deutschen Archäologischen Instituts,
        Athenische Abteilung.
   ISTANBUL. Mitteilungen des deutschen Archäologischen Instituts,
        Abteilung Istanbul.
   MADRID. Mitteilungen des deutschen Archäologischen Instituts,
        Madrider Abteilung.
   ROME. Mitteilungen des deutschen Archäologischen Instituts,
        Römische Abteilung.
In addition to the above, there are miscellaneous collections of works
issued by the German Archaeological Institute:
(1) Denkmäler antiker Architektur, 10 vols. 1932-1962.
(2) Studien zur spätantiken Kunstgeschichte, 12 vols., ed. H. Lietzmann

and G. Rodenwaldt. 1925-1941.

The Archaeological Society of Berlin publishes yearly a volume of
essays on various topics; this is called the Winckelmannsprogramm
der Archäologischen Gesellschaft zu Berlin, 125 vols. Still in
progress; latest volume published in 1973.

The Corpus Vasorum Antiquorum for Germany contains 28 fasicules.

The most important French excavation reports are:

(1) DELOS. Exploration archéologique de Délos, 30 fasicules. 1909 --.

(2) DELPHI. Fouilles de Delphes, 5 vols., 18 fasicules. 1902 --.

(3) LINDOS. Lindos. Fouilles et recherches, 3 vols. 1902-1914.

(4) MALLIA. Fouilles exécutées à Mallia, 9 vols. 1922 --.

(5) THASOS. Études Thasiennes, 8 vols. 1944 --.

Progress reports and preliminary notices of results are published in
the annual Bulletin de Correspondence Hellénique. The Corpus Vasorum
Antiquorum for France now contains 21 fasicules.

<u>ADDENDA</u>.

The following books were published too late to be included in
main body of the text:

<u>Section I, p.4</u>.

BRAY, W. and TRUMP, D. <u>The Penguin dictionary of archaeology</u>.
Baltimore: Penguin Books 1972. Pp. 269; 211 figs.; 6 maps.
$2.65 paper.
First published in 1970.
An excellent dictionary of archaeology covering the important
sites around the world. Yet, the title is somewhat misleading.
The dictionary is raelly one of prehistoric archaeology;
classical and medieval archaeology are not covered. Furthermore,
since the authors are English, there is a heavy emphasis on
British archaeology of all periods. B.

<u>Section II, p.15</u>.

FAGAN, B.M. <u>In the beginning: an introduction to archaeology</u>, 2nd ed.
Boston: Little, Brown and Co. 1975. Pp. 410; 155 figs. $10.95 cloth.
An excellent survey of the aims, methods, and techniques of
archaeology; highly recommended as a textbook. A.

<u>Section IV, p.44-5</u>.

EXCAVATIONS <u>of the Athenian Agora: picture books</u>. Princeton:
American School of Classical Studies. Pp. 32. Paper.
No.14. <u>Graffiti in the Athenian Agora</u>. (1974) $1.00.